SANDERS OF THE RIVER

BY
EDGAR WALLACE

Republished 2023

D1706548

CONTENTS.

SANDERS OF THE RIVER.
CHAPTER I.
THE EDUCATION OF THE KING.

Mr. Commissioner Sanders had graduated to West Central Africa by such easy stages that he did not realise when his acquaintance with the back lands began. Long before he was called upon by the British Government to keep a watchful eye upon some quarter of a million cannibal folk, who ten years before had regarded white men as we regard the unicorn; he had met the Basuto, the Zulu, the Fingo, the Pondo, Matabele, Mashona, Barotse, Hottentot, and Bechuana. Then curiosity and interest took him westward and northward, and he met the Angola folk, then northward to the Congo, westward to the Masai, and finally, by way of the Pigmy people, he came to his own land.

Now, there is a subtle difference between all these races, a difference that only such men as Sanders know.

It is not necessarily a variety of colour, though some are brown and some yellow, and some—a very few—jet black. The difference is in character. By Sanders' code you trusted all natives up to the same point, as you trust children, with a few notable exceptions. The Zulu were men, the Basuto were men, yet childlike in their grave faith. The black men who wore the fez were subtle, but trustworthy; but the browny men of the Gold Coast, who talked English, wore European clothing, and called one another "Mr.," were Sanders' pet abomination.

Living so long with children of a larger growth, it follows that he absorbed many of their childlike qualities. Once, on furlough in London, a confidence trick was played on him, and only his natural honesty pulled him out of a ridiculous scrape. For, when the gold-brick man produced his dull metal ingot, all Sanders' moral nerves stood endways, and he ran the confiding "bunco steerer" to the nearest station, charging him, to the astonishment of a sorely-puzzled policeman, with "I.G.B.," which means illicit gold buying. Sanders did not doubt that the ingot was gold, but he was equally certain that the gold was not honestly come by. His surprise when he found that the "gold" was gold-leaf imposed upon the lead of commerce was pathetic.

You may say of Sanders that he was a statesman, which means that he had no exaggerated opinion of the value of individual human life. When he saw a dead leaf on the plant of civilisation, he plucked it off, or a weed growing with his "flowers" he pulled it up, not stopping to consider the weed's equal right to life. When a man, whether he was *capita* or slave, by his bad example endangered the peace of his country, Sanders fell upon him. In their unregenerate days, the Isisi called him "Ogani Isisi," which means "The Little Butcher Bird," and certainly in that time Sanders was prompt to hang. He governed a people three hundred miles beyond the fringe of civilisation. Hesitation to act, delay in awarding punishment, either of these two things would have been mistaken for weakness amongst a people who had neither power to reason, nor will to excuse, nor any large charity.

In the land which curves along the borders of Togo the people understand punishment to mean pain and death, and nothing else counts. There was a foolish Commissioner who was a great humanitarian, and he went up to Akasava—which is the name of this land—and tried moral suasion.

It was a raiding palaver. Some of the people of Akasava had crossed the river to Ochori and stolen women and goats, and I believe there was a man or two killed, but that is unimportant. The goats and the women were alive, and cried aloud for vengeance. They cried so loud that down at headquarters they were heard and Mr. Commissioner Niceman—that was not his name, but it will serve—went up to see what all the noise was about. He found the Ochori people very angry, but more frightened.

"If," said their spokesman, "they will return our goats, they may keep the women, because the goats are very valuable."

So Mr. Commissioner Niceman had a long, long palaver that lasted days and days, with the chief of the Akasava people and his councillors, and in the end moral suasion triumphed, and the people promised on a certain day, at a certain hour, when the moon was in such a quarter and the tide at such a height, the women should be returned and the goats also.

So Mr. Niceman returned to headquarters, swelling with admiration for himself and wrote a long report about his genius and his administrative abilities, and his knowledge of the native, which was afterwards published in Blue Book (Africa) 7943-96.

It so happened that Mr. Niceman immediately afterwards went home to England on furlough, so that he did not hear the laments and woeful wailings of the Ochori folk when they did not get their women or their goats.

Sanders, working round the Isisi River, with ten Houssas and an attack of malaria, got a helio message:

"Go Akasava and settle that infernal woman palaver.—ADMINISTRATION."

So Sanders girded up his loins, took 25 grains of quinine, and leaving his good work—he was searching for M'Beli, the witch-doctor, who had poisoned a friend—trekked across country for the Akasava.

In the course of time he came to the city and was met by the chief.

"What about these women?" he asked.

"We will have a palaver," said the chief. "I will summon my headmen and my councillors."

"Summon nothing," said Sanders shortly. "Send back the women and the goats you stole from the Ochori."

"Master," said the chief, "at full moon, which is our custom, when the tide is so, and all signs of gods and devils are propitious, I will do as you bid."

"Chief," said Sanders, tapping the ebony chest of the other with the thin end of his walking-stick, "moon and river, gods or devils, those women and the goats go back to the Ochori folk by sunset, or I tie you to a tree and flog you till you bleed."

4

"Master," said the chief, "the women shall be returned."

"And the goats," said Sanders.

"As to the goats," said the chief airily, "they are dead, having been killed for a feast."

"You will bring them back to life," said Sanders.

"Master, do you think I am a magician?" asked the chief of the Akasava.

"I think you are a liar," said Sanders impartially, and there the palaver finished.

That night goats and women returned to the Ochori, and Sanders prepared to depart.

He took aside the chief, not desiring to put shame upon him or to weaken his authority.

"Chief," he said, "it is a long journey to Akasava, and I am a man fulfilling many tasks. I desire that you do not cause me any further journey to this territory."

"Master," said the chief truthfully, "I never wish to see you again."

Sanders smiled aside, collected his ten Houssas, and went back to the Isisi River to continue his search for M'Beli.

It was not a nice search for many causes, and there was every reason to believe, too, that the king of Isisi himself was the murderer's protector. Confirmation of this view came one morning when Sanders, encamped by the Big River, was taking a breakfast of tinned milk and toast. There arrived hurriedly Sato-Koto, the brother of the king, in great distress of mind, for he was a fugitive from the king's wrath. He babbled forth all manner of news, in much of which Sanders took no interest whatever. But what he said of the witch-doctor who lived in the king's shadow was very interesting indeed, and Sanders sent a messenger to headquarters, and, as it transpired, headquarters despatched in the course of time Mr. Niceman—who by this time had returned from furlough—to morally "suade" the king of the Isisi.

From such evidence as we have been able to collect it is evident that the king was not in a melting mood. It is an indisputable fact that poor Niceman's head, stuck on a pole before the king's hut, proclaimed the king's high spirits.

H.M.S. *St. George*, H.M.S. *Thrush*, H.M.S. *Philomel*, H.M.S. *Phoebe* sailed from Simonstown, and H.M.S. *Dwarf* came down from Sierra Leone *hec dum*, and in less than a month after the king killed his guest he wished he hadn't.

Headquarters sent Sanders to clear up the political side of the mess.

He was shown round what was left of the king's city by the flag-lieutenant of the *St. George.*

"I am afraid," said that gentleman, apologetically, "I am afraid that you will have to dig out a new king; we've rather killed the old one."

Sanders nodded.

"I shall not go into mourning," he said.

There was no difficulty in finding candidates for the vacant post. Sato-Koto, the dead king's brother, expressed his willingness to assume the cares of office with commendable promptitude.

"What do you say?" asked the admiral, commanding the expedition.

"I say no, sir," said Sanders, without hesitation. "The king has a son, a boy of nine; the kingship must be his. As for Sato-Koto, he shall be regent at pleasure."

And so it was arranged, Sato-Koto sulkily assenting.

They found the new king hidden in the woods with the women folk, and he tried to bolt, but Sanders caught him and led him back to the city by the ear.

"My boy," he said kindly, "how do people call you?"

"Peter, master," whimpered the wriggling lad; "in the fashion of the white people."

"Very well," said Sanders, "you shall be King Peter, and rule this country wisely and justly according to custom and the law. And you shall do hurt to none, and put shame on none nor shall you kill or raid or do any of the things that make life worth living, and if you break loose, may the Lord help you!"

Thus was King Peter appointed monarch of the Isisi people, and Sanders went back to head-quarters with the little army of bluejackets and Houssas, for M'Beli, the witch-doctor, had been slain at the taking of the city, and Sanders' work was finished.

The story of the taking of Isisi village, and the crowning of the young king, was told in the London newspapers, and lost nothing in the telling. It was so described by the special correspondents, who accompanied the expedition, that many dear old ladies of Bayswater wept, and many dear young ladies of Mayfair said: "How sweet!" and the outcome of the many emotions which the description evoked was the sending out from England of Miss Clinton Calbraith, who was an M.A., and unaccountably pretty.

She came out to "mother" the orphan king, to be a mentor and a friend. She paid her own passage, but the books which she brought and the school paraphernalia that filled two large packing cases were subscribed for by the tender readers of *Tiny Toddlers*, a magazine for infants. Sanders met her on the landing-stage, being curious to see what a white woman looked like.

He put a hut at her disposal and sent the wife of his coast clerk to look after her.

"And now, Miss Calbraith," he said, at dinner that night, "what do you expect to do with Peter?"

She tilted her pretty chin in the air reflectively.

"We shall start with the most elementary of lessons—the merest kindergarten, and gradually work up. I shall teach him calisthenics, a little botany—Mr. Sanders, you're laughing."

"No, I wasn't," he hastened to assure her; "I always make a face like that—er—in the evening. But tell me this—do you speak the language—Swaheli, Bomongo, Fingi?"

"That will be a difficulty," she said thoughtfully.

"Will you take my advice?" he asked.

"Why, yes."

"Well, learn the language." She nodded. "Go home and learn it." She frowned. "It will take you about twenty-five years."

"Mr. Sanders," she said, not without dignity, "you are pulling—you are making fun of me."

"Heaven forbid!" said Sanders piously, "that I should do anything so wicked."

The end of the story, so far as Miss Clinton Calbraith was concerned, was that she went to Isisi, stayed three days, and came back incoherent.

"He is not a child!" she said wildly; "he is—a—a little devil!"

"So I should say," said Sanders philosophically.

"A king? It is disgraceful! He lives in a mud hut and wears no clothes. If I'd known!"

"A child of nature," said Sanders blandly. "You didn't expect a sort of Louis Quinze, did you?"

"I don't know what I expected," she said desperately; "but it was impossible to stay—quite impossible."

"Obviously," murmured Sanders.

"Of course, I knew he would be black," she went on; "and I knew that—oh, it was too horrid!"

"The fact of it is, my dear young lady," said Sanders, "Peter wasn't as picturesque as you imagined him; he wasn't the gentle child with pleading eyes; and he lives messy—is that it?"

This was not the only attempt ever made to educate Peter. Months afterwards, when Miss Calbraith had gone home and was busily writing her famous book, "Alone in Africa: by an English Gentlewoman," Sanders heard of another educative raid. Two members of an Ethiopian mission came into Isisi by the back way. The Ethiopian mission is made up of Christian black men, who, very properly, basing their creed upon Holy Writ, preach the gospel of Equality. A black man is as good as a white man any day of the week, and infinitely better on Sundays if he happens to be a member of the Reformed Ethiopian Church.

They came to Isisi and achieved instant popularity, for the kind of talk they provided was very much to the liking of Sato-Koto and the king's councillors.

Sanders sent for the missioners. The first summons they refused to obey, but they came on the second occasion, because the message Sanders sent was at once peremptory and ominous.

They came to headquarters, two cultured American negroes of good address and refined conversation. They spoke English faultlessly, and were in every sense perfect gentlemen.

"We cannot understand the character of your command," said one, "which savours somewhat of interference with the liberty of the subject."

"You'll understand me better," said Sanders, who knew his men, "when I tell you that I cannot allow you to preach sedition to my people."

"Sedition, Mr. Sanders!" said the negro in shocked tones. "That is a grave charge."

Sanders took a paper from a pigeon-hole in his desk; the interview took place in his office.

"On such a date," he said, "you said this, and this, and that."

In other words he accused them of overstepping the creed of Equality and encroaching upon the borderland of political agitation.

"Lies!" said the elder of the two, without hesitation.

"Truth or lies," he said, "you go no more to Isisi."

"Would you have the heathen remain in darkness?" asked the man, in reproach. "Is the light we kindle too bright, master?"

"No," said Sanders, "but a bit too warm."

So he committed the outrage of removing the Ethiopians from the scene of their earnest labours, in consequence of which questions were asked in Parliament.

Then the chief of the Akasava people—an old friend—took a hand in the education of King Peter. Akasava adjoins that king's territory, and the chief came to give hints in military affairs.

He came with drums a-beating, with presents of fish and bananas and salt.

"You are a great king!" he said to the sleepy-eyed boy who sat on a stool of state, regarding him with open-mouthed interest. "When you walk the world shakes at your tread; the mighty river that goes flowing down to the big water parts asunder at your word, the trees of the forest shiver, and the beasts go slinking to cover when your mightiness goes abroad."

"Oh, ko, ko!" giggled the king, pleasantly tickled.

"The white men fear you," continued the chief of the Akasava; "they tremble and hide at your roar."

Sato-Koto, standing at the king's elbow, was a practical man.

"What seek ye, chief?" he asked, cutting short the compliments.

So the chief told him of a land peopled by cowards, rich with the treasures of the earth, goats, and women.

"Why do you not take them yourself?" demanded the regent.

"Because I am a slave," said the chief; "the slave of Sandi, who would beat me. But you, lord, are of the great; being king's headman, Sandi would not beat you because of your greatness."

There followed a palaver, which lasted two days.

"I shall have to do something with Peter," wrote Sanders despairingly to the Administrator; "the little beggar has gone on the war-path against those unfortunate Ochori. I should be glad if you would send me a hundred men, a

Maxim, and a bundle of rattan canes; I'm afraid I must attend to Peter's education myself."

"Lord, did I not speak the truth?" said the Akasava chief in triumph. "Sandi has done nothing! Behold, we have wasted the city of the Ochori, and taken their treasure, and the white man is dumb because of your greatness! Let us wait till the moon comes again, and I will show you another city."

"You are a great man," bleated the king, "and some day you shall build your hut in the shadow of my palace."

"On that day," said the chief, with splendid resignation, "I shall die of joy."

When the moon had waxed and waned and come again, a pencilled silver hoop of light in the eastern sky, the Isisi warriors gathered with spear and broad-bladed sword, with *ingola* on their bodies, and clay in their hair.

They danced a great dance by the light of a huge fire, and all the women stood round, clapping their hands rhythmically.

In the midst of this there arrived a messenger in a canoe, who prostrated himself before the king, saying:

"Master, one day's march from here is Sandi; he has with him five score of soldiers and the brass gun which says: 'Ha-ha-ha-ha-ha!'"

A silence reigned in court circles, which was broken by the voice of the Akasava chief.

"I think I will go home," he said. "I have a feeling of sickness; also, it is the season when my goats have their young."

"Do not be afraid," said Sato-Koto brutally. "The king's shadow is over you, and he is so mighty that the earth shakes at his tread, and the waters of the big river part at his footfall; also, the white men fear him."

"Nevertheless," said the chief, with some agitation, "I must go, for my youngest son is sickening with fever, and calls all the time for me."

"Stay!" said the regent, and there was no mistaking his tone.

Sanders did not come the next day, nor the next. He was moving leisurely, traversing a country where many misunderstandings existed that wanted clearing up. When he arrived, having sent a messenger ahead to carry the news of his arrival, he found the city peaceably engaged.

The women were crushing corn, the men smoking, the little children playing and sprawling about the streets.

He halted at the outskirts of the city, on a hillock that commanded the main street, and sent for the regent.

"Why must I send for you?" he asked. "Why does the king remain in his city when I come? This is shame."

"Master," said Sato-Koto, "it is not fitting that a great king should so humble himself."

Sanders was neither amused nor angry. He was dealing with a rebellious people, and his own fine feelings were as nothing to the peace of the land.

"It would seem that the king has had bad advisers," he reflected aloud, and Sato-Koto shuffled uneasily.

"Go, now, and tell the king to come—for I am his friend."

The regent departed, but returned again alone.

"Lord, he will not come," he said sullenly.

"Then I will go to him," said Sanders.

King Peter, sitting before his hut, greeted Mr. Commissioner with downcast eyes.

Sanders' soldiers, spread in a semi-circle before the hut, kept the rabble at bay.

"King," said Sanders—he carried in his hand a rattan cane of familiar shape, and as he spoke he whiffled it in the air, making a little humming noise—"stand up!"

"Wherefore?" said Sato-Koto.

"That you shall see," said Sanders.

The king rose reluctantly, and Sanders grabbed him by the scruff of his neck.

Swish!

The cane caught him most undesirably, and he sprang into the air with a yell.

Swish, swish, swish!

Yelling and dancing, throwing out wild hands to ward off the punishment, King Peter blubbered for mercy.

"Master!" Sato-Koto, his face distorted with rage, reached for his spear.

"Shoot that man if he interferes," said Sanders, without releasing the king.

The regent saw the levelled rifles and stepped back hastily.

"Now," said Sanders, throwing down the cane, "now we will play a little game."

"Wow-wow—oh, ko!" sobbed his majesty.

"I go back to the forest," said Sanders. "By and by a messenger shall come to you, saying that the Commissioner is on his way. Do you understand?"

"Yi-hi!" sobbed the king.

"Then will you go out with your councillors and your old men and await my coming according to custom. Is that clear?"

"Ye-es, master," whimpered the boy.

"Very good," said Sanders, and withdrew his troops.

In half an hour came a grave messenger to the king, and the court went out to the little hill to welcome the white man.

This was the beginning of King Peter's education, for thus was he taught obedience.

Sanders went into residence in the town of Isisi, and held court.

"Sato-Koto," he said on the second day, "do you know the village of Ikan?"

"Yes, master; it is two days' journey into the bush."

Sanders nodded.

"You will take your wives, your children, your servants, and your possessions to the village of Ikan, there to stay until I give you leave to return. The palaver is finished."

Next came the chief of the Akasava, very ill at ease.

"Lord, if any man says I did you wrong, he lies," said the chief.

"Then I am a liar!" said Sanders. "For I say that you are an evil man, full of cunning."

"If it should be," said the chief, "that you order me to go to my village as you have ordered Sato-Koto, I will go, since he who is my father is not pleased with me."

"That I order," said Sanders; "also, twenty strokes with a stick, for the good of your soul. Furthermore, I would have you remember that down by Tembeli on the great river there is a village where men labour in chains because they have been unfaithful to the Government and have practised abominations."

So the chief of the Akasava people went out to punishment.

There were other matters requiring adjustment, but they were of a minor character, and when these were all settled to the satisfaction of Sanders, but by no means to the satisfaction of the subjects, the Commissioner turned his attention to the further education of the king.

"Peter," he said, "to-morrow when the sun comes up I go back to my own village, leaving you without councillors."

"Master, how may I do without councillors, since I am a young boy?" asked the king, crestfallen and chastened.

"By saying to yourself when a man calls for justice: 'If I were this man how should I desire the king's justice?'"

The boy looked unhappy.

"I am very young," he repeated; "and to-day there come many from outlying villages seeking redress against their enemies."

"Very good," said Sanders. "To-day I will sit at the king's right hand and learn of his wisdom."

The boy stood on one leg in his embarrassment, and eyed Sanders askance.

There is a hillock behind the town. A worn path leads up to it, and a-top is a thatched hut without sides. From this hillock you see the broad river with its sandy shoals, where the crocodiles sleep with open mouth; you see the rising ground toward Akasava, hills that rise one on top of the other, covered with a tangle of vivid green. In this house sits the king in judgment, beckoning the litigants forward. Sato-Koto was wont to stand by the king, bartering justice.

To-day Sato-Koto was preparing to depart and Sanders sat by the king's side.

There were indeed many litigants.

There was a man who had bought a wife, giving no less than a thousand rods and two bags of salt for her. He had lived for three months with her, when she departed from his house.

"Because," said the man philosophically, "she had a lover. Therefore, Mighty Sun of Wisdom, I desire the return of my rods and my salt."

"What say you?" said Sanders.

The king wriggled uncomfortably.

"What says the father?" he said hesitatingly, and Sanders nodded.

"That is a wise question," he approved, and called the father, a voluble and an eager old man.

"Now, king," he said hurriedly, "I sold this woman, my daughter; how might I know her mind? Surely I fulfil my contract when the woman goes to the man. How shall a father control when a husband fails?"

Sanders looked at the king again, and the boy drew a long breath.

"It would seem, M'bleni, that the woman, your daughter, lived many years in your hut, and if you do not know her mind you are either a great fool or she is a cunning one. Therefore, I judge that you sold this woman knowing her faults. Yet the husband might accept some risk also. You shall take back your daughter and return 500 rods and a bag of salt, and if it should be that your daughter marries again, you shall pay one-half of her dowry to this man."

Very, very slowly he gave judgment, hesitatingly, anxiously, glancing now and again to the white man for his approval.

"That was good," said Sanders, and called forward another pleader.

"Lord king," said the new plaintiff, "a man has put an evil curse on me and my family, so that they sicken."

Here was a little poser for the little judge, and he puzzled the matter out in silence, Sanders offering no help.

"How does he curse you?" at last asked the king.

"With the curse of death," said the complainant in a hushed voice.

"Then you shall curse him also," said the king, "and it shall be a question of whose curse is the stronger."

Sanders grinned behind his hand, and the king, seeing the smile, smiled also.

From here onward Peter's progress was a rapid one, and there came to headquarters from time to time stories of a young king who was a Solomon in judgment.

So wise he was (who knew of the formula he applied to each case?), so beneficent, so peaceable, that the chief of the Akasava, from whom was periodically due, took advantage of the gentle administration, and sent neither corn nor fish nor grain. He did this after a journey to far-away Ikan, where he met the king's uncle, Sato-Koto, and agreed upon common action. Since the crops were good, the king passed the first fault, but the second tribute became due, and neither Akasava nor Ikan sent, and the people of Isisi, angry at the insolence, murmured, and the king sat down in the loneliness of his hut to think upon a course which was just and effective.

"I really am sorry to bother you," wrote Sanders to the Administrator again, "but I shall have to borrow your Houssas for the Isisi country. There has been a tribute palaver, and Peter went down to Ikan and wiped up his uncle; he filled in his spare time by giving the Akasava the worst licking they have ever had. I thoroughly approve of all that Peter has done, because I feel that he is actuated only by the keenest sense of justice and a desire to do the right thing at the right time—and it was time Sato-Koto was killed—though I shall have to reprimand Peter for the sake of appearances. The Akasava chief is in the bush, hiding."

Peter came back to his capital after his brief but strenuous campaign, leaving behind him two territories that were all the better for his visit, though somewhat sore.

The young king brought together his old men, his witch-doctors, and other notabilities.

"By all the laws of white men," he said, "I have done wrong to Sandi, because he has told me I must not fight, and, behold, I have destroyed my uncle, who was a dog, and I have driven the chief of the Akasava into the forest. But Sandi told me also that I must do what was just, and that I have done according to my lights, for I have destroyed a man who put my people to shame. Now, it seems to me that there is only one thing to do, and that is to go to Sandi, telling the truth and asking him to judge."

"Lord king," said the oldest of his councillors, "what if Sandi puts you to the chain-gang?"

"That is with to-morrow," quoth the king, and gave orders for preparations to be made for departure.

Half-way to headquarters the two met; King Peter going down and Sanders coming up. And here befell the great incident.

No word was spoken of Peter's fault before sunset; but when blue smoke arose from the fires of Houssa and warrior, and the little camp in the forest clearing was all a-chatter, Sanders took the king's arm and led him along the forest path.

15

Peter told his tale and Sanders listened.

"And what of the chief of the Akasava?" he asked.

"Master," said the king, "he fled to the forest cursing me, and with him went many bad men."

Sanders nodded again gravely.

They talked of many things till the sun threw long shadows, and then they turned to retrace their footsteps. They were within half a mile of the camp and the faint noise of men laughing, and the faint scent of fires burning came to them, when the chief of the Akasava stepped out from behind a tree and stood directly in their path. With him were some eight fighting men fully armed.

"Lord king," said the chief of the Akasava, "I have been waiting for you."

The king made neither movement nor reply, but Sanders reached for his revolver.

His hand closed on the butt, when something struck him and he went down like a log.

"Now we will kill the king of the Isisi, and the white man also." The voice was the chief's, but Sanders was not taking any particular interest in the conversation, because there was a hive of wild bees buzzing in his head, and a maze of pain; he felt sick.

"If you kill me it is little matter," said the king's voice, "because there are many men who can take my place; but if you slay Sandi, you slay the father of the people, and none can replace him."

"He whipped you, little king," said the chief of the Akasava mockingly.

"I would throw him into the river," said a strange voice after a long interval; "thus shall no trace be found of him, and no man will lay his death to our door."

"What of the king?" said another. Then came a crackling of twigs and the voices of men.

"They are searching," whispered a voice. "King, if you speak I will kill you now."

"Kill!" said the young king's even voice, and shouted, "Oh, M'sabo! Beteli! Sandi is here!"

That was all Sandi heard.

Two days later he sat up in bed and demanded information. There was a young doctor with him when he woke, who had providentially arrived from headquarters.

"The king?" he hesitated. "Well, they finished the king, but he saved your life. I suppose you know that?"

Sanders said "Yes" without emotion.

"A plucky little beggar," suggested the doctor.

"Very," said Sanders. Then: "Did they catch the chief of the Akasava?"

"Yes; he was so keen on finishing you that he delayed his bolting. The king threw himself on you and covered your body."

"That will do."

Sanders' voice was harsh and his manner brusque at the best of times, but now his rudeness was brutal.

"Just go out of the hut, doctor—I want to sleep."

He heard the doctor move, heard the rattle of the "chick" at the hut door, then he turned his face to the wall and wept.

CHAPTER II.
KEEPERS OF THE STONE.

There is a people who live at Ochori in the big African forest on the Ikeli River, who are called in the native tongue "The Keepers of the Stone."

There is a legend that years and years ago, *cala-cala*, there was a strange, flat stone, "inscribed with the marks of the devils" (so the grave native story-teller puts it), which was greatly worshipped and prized, partly for its magic powers, and partly because of the two ghosts who guarded it.

It was a fetish of peculiar value to the mild people who lived in the big forest, but the Akasava, who are neither mild nor reverential, and being, moreover, in need of gods, swooped down upon the Ochori one red morning and came away with this wonderful stone and other movables. Presumably, the "ghosts of brass" went also. It was a great business, securing the stone, for it was set in a grey slab in the solid rock, and many spear-heads were broken before it could be wrenched from its place. But in the end it was taken away, and for several years it was the boast of the Akasava that they derived much benefit from this sacred possession. Then of a sudden the stone disappeared, and with it all the good fortune of its owners. For the vanishing of the stone coincided with the arrival of British rule, and it was a bad thing for the Akasava.

There came in these far-off days ('95?) a ridiculous person in white with an escort of six soldiers. He brought a message of peace and good fellowship, and talked of a new king and a new law. The Akasava listened in dazed wonderment, but when they recovered they cut off his head, also the heads of the escort. It seemed to be the only thing to do under the circumstances.

Then one morning the Akasava people woke to find the city full of strange white folk, who had come swiftly up the river in steamboats. There were too many to quarrel with, so the people sat quiet, a little frightened and very curious, whilst two black soldiers strapped the hands and feet of the Akasava chief prior to hanging him by the neck till he was dead.

Nor did the bad luck of the people end here; there came a lean year, when the manioc[1] root was bad and full of death-water, when goats died, and crops were spoilt by an unexpected hurricane. There was always a remedy at hand for a setback of this kind. If you have not the thing you require, go and take it. So, following precedents innumerable, the Akasava visited the Ochori, taking away much grain, and leaving behind dead men and men who prayed for death. In the course of time the white men came with their steamboats, their little brass guns, and the identical block and tackle, which they fastened to the identical tree and utilised in the inevitable manner.

"It appears," said the new chief—who was afterwards hanged for the killing of the king of the Isisi—"that the white man's law is made to allow weak men to triumph at the expense of the strong. This seems foolish, but it will be well to humour them."

His first act was to cut down the hanging-tree—it was too conspicuous and too significant. Then he set himself to discover the cause of all the trouble which had come upon the Akasava. The cause required little appreciation. The great stone had been stolen, as he well knew, and the remedy resolved itself into a question of discovering the thief. The wretched Ochori were suspect.

"If we go to them," said the chief of the Akasava thoughtfully, "killing them very little, but rather burning them, so that they told where this godstone was hidden, perhaps the Great Ones would forgive us."

"In my young days," said an aged councillor, "when evil men would not tell where stolen things were buried, we put hot embers in their hands and bound them tightly."

"That is a good way," approved another old man, wagging his head applaudingly; "also to tie men in the path of the soldier-ants has been known to make them talkative."

"Yet we may not go up against the Ochori for many reasons," said the chief; "the principal of which is that if the stone be with them we shall not overcome them owing to the two ghosts—though I do not remember that the ghosts were very potent in the days when the stone was with us," he added, not without hope.

The little raid which followed and the search for the stone are told briefly in official records. The search was fruitless, and the Akasava folk must needs content themselves with such picking as came to hand.

Of how Mr. Niceman, the deputy commissioner, and then Sanders himself, came up, I have already told. That was long ago, as the natives say, *cala-cala*, and many things happened subsequently that put from the minds of the people all thought of the stone.

In course of time the chief of the Akasava died the death for various misdoings, and peace came to the land that fringes Togo.

Sanders has been surprised twice in his life. Once was at Ikeli, which in the native tongue means "little river." It is not a little river at all, but, on the contrary, a broad, strong, sullen stream that swirls and eddies and foams as it swings the corner of its tortuous course seaward. Sanders sat on a deck-chair placed under the awning of his tiny steamer, and watched the river go rushing past. He was a contented man, for the land was quiet and the crops were good. Nor was there any crime.

There was sleeping sickness at Bofabi, and beri-beri at Akasava, and in the Isisi country somebody had discovered a new god, and, by all accounts that came down river, they worshipped him night and day.

He was not bothering about new gods, because gods of any kind were a beneficent asset. Milini, the new king of the Isisi, had sent him word:

"Master," said his mouthpiece, the messenger, "this new god lives in a box which is borne upon the shoulders of priests. It is so long and so wide, and there are four sockets in which the poles fit, and the god inside is a very strong one, and full of pride."

"Ko, ko!" said Sanders, with polite interest, "tell the lord king, your master, that so long as this god obeys the law, he may live in the Isisi country, paying no tax.

But if he tells the young men to go fighting, I shall come with a much stronger god, who will eat your god up. The palaver is finished."

Sanders, with his feet stretched out on the rail of the boat, thought of the new god idly. When was it that the last had come? There was one in the N'Gombi country years ago, a sad god who lived in a hut which no man dare approach; there was another god who came with thunder demanding sacrifice—human sacrifice. This was an exceptionally bad god, and had cost the British Government six hundred thousand pounds, because there was fighting in the bush and a country unsettled. But, in the main, the gods were good, doing harm to none, for it is customary for new gods to make their appearance after the crops are gathered, and before the rainy season sets in.

So Sanders thought, sitting in the shade of a striped awning on the foredeck of the little *Zaire*.

The next day, before the sun came up, he turned the nose of the steamer up-stream, being curious as to the welfare of the shy Ochori folk, who lived too near the Akasava for comfort, and, moreover, needed nursing. Very slow was the tiny steamer's progress, for the current was strong against her. After two days' travel Sanders got into Lukati, where young Carter had a station.

The deputy commissioner came down to the beach in his pyjamas, with a big pith helmet on the back of his head, and greeted his chief boisterously.

"Well?" said Sanders; and Carter told him all the news. There was a land palaver at Ebibi; Otabo, of Bofabi, had died of the sickness; there were two leopards worrying the outlying villages, and——

"Heard about the Isisi god?" he asked suddenly; and Sanders said that he had.

"It's an old friend of yours," said Carter. "My people tell me that this old god-box contains the stone of the Ochori."

"Oh!" said Sanders, with sudden interest.

He breakfasted with his subordinate, inspected his little garrison of thirty, visited his farm, admired his sweet potatoes, and patronised his tomatoes.

Then he went back to the boat and wrote a short dispatch in the tiniest of handwriting on the flimsiest of paper slips. "In case!" said Sanders.

"Bring me 14," he said to his servant, and Abiboo came back to him soon with a pigeon in his hand.

"Now, little bird," said Sanders, carefully rolling his letter round the red leg of the tiny courier and fastening it with a rubber band, "you've got two hundred miles to fly before sunrise to-morrow—and 'ware hawks!"

Then he gathered the pigeon in his hand, walked with it to the stern of the boat, and threw it into the air.

His crew of twelve men were sitting about their cooking-pot—that pot which everlastingly boils.

"Yoka!" he called, and his half-naked engineer came bounding down the slope.

"Steam," said Sanders; "get your wood aboard; I am for Isisi."

There was no doubt at all that this new god was an extremely powerful one. Three hours from the city the *Zaire* came up to a long canoe with four men standing at their paddles singing dolefully. Sanders remembered that he had passed a village where women, their bodies decked with green leaves, wailed by the river's edge.

He slowed down till he came abreast of the canoe, and saw a dead man lying stark in the bottom.

"Where go you with this body?" he asked.

"To Isisi, lord," was the answer.

"The middle river and the little islands are places for the dead," said Sanders brusquely. "It is folly to take the dead to the living."

"Lord," said the man who spoke, "at Isisi lives a god who breathes life; this man"—he pointed downwards—"is my brother, and he died very suddenly because of a leopard. So quickly he died that he could not tell us where he had hidden his rods and his salt. Therefore we take him to Isisi, that the new god may give him just enough life to make his relations comfortable."

"The middle river," said Sanders quietly, and pointed to such a lone island, all green with tangled vegetation, as might make a burying ground. "What is your name?"

"Master, my name is N'Kema," said the man sullenly.

"Go, then, N'Kema," he said, and kept the steamer slow ahead whilst he watched the canoe turn its blunt nose to the island and disembark its cargo.

Then he rang the engines full ahead, steered clear of a sandbank, and regained the fairway.

He was genuinely concerned.

The stone was something exceptional in fetishes, needing delicate handling. That the stone existed, he knew. There were legends innumerable about it; and an explorer had, in the early days, seen it through his glasses. Also the "ghosts clad in brass" he had heard about—these fantastic and warlike shades who made peaceable men go out to battle—all except the Ochori, who were never warlike, and whom no number of ghosts could incite to deeds of violence.

You will have remarked that Sanders took native people seriously, and that, I remark in passing, is the secret of good government. To him, ghosts were factors, and fetishes potent possibilities. A man who knew less would have been amused, but Sanders was not amused, because he had a great responsibility. He arrived at the city of Isisi in the afternoon, and observed, even at a distance, that something unusual was occurring. The crowd of women and children that the arrival of the Commissioner usually attracted did not gather as he swung in from mid-stream and followed the water-path that leads to shoal.

Only the king and a handful of old men awaited him, and the king was nervous and in trouble.

"Lord," he blurted, "I am no king in this city because of the new god; the people are assembled on the far side of the hill, and there they sit night and day watching the god in the box."

Sanders bit his lip thoughtfully, and said nothing.

"Last night," said the king, "'The Keepers of the Stone' appeared walking through the village."

He shivered, and the sweat stood in big beads on his forehead, for a ghost is a terrible thing.

"All this talk of keepers of stones is folly," said Sanders calmly; "they have been seen by your women and your unblooded boys."

"Lord, I saw them myself," said the king simply; and Sanders was staggered, for the king was a sane man.

"The devil you have!" said Sanders in English; then, "What manner of ghost were these?"

"Lord," said the king, "they were white of face, like your greatness. They wore brass upon their heads and brass upon their breasts. Their legs were bare, but upon the lower legs was brass again."

"Any kind of ghost is hard enough to believe," said Sanders irritably, "but a brass ghost I will not have at any price." He spoke English again, as was his practice when he talked to himself, and the king stood silent, not understanding him.

"What else?" said Sanders.

"They had swords," continued the chief, "such as the elephant-hunters of the N'Gombi people carry. Broad and short, and on their arms were shields."

Sanders was nonplussed.

"And they cry 'war,'" said the chief. "This is the greatest shame of all, for my young men dance the death dance and streak their bodies with paint and talk boastfully."

"Go to your hut," said Sanders; "presently I will come and join you."

He thought and thought, smoking one black cigar after another, then he sent for Abiboo, his servant.

"Abiboo," he said, "by my way of thinking, I have been a good master to you."

"That is so, lord," said Abiboo.

"Now I will trust you to go amongst my crew discovering their gods. If I ask them myself, they will lie to me out of politeness, inventing this god and that, thinking they please me."

Abiboo chose the meal hour, when the sun had gone out and the world was grey and the trees motionless. He came back with the information as Sanders was drinking his second cup of coffee in the loneliness of the tiny deck-house.

"Master," he reported, "three men worship no god whatever, three more have especial family fetishes, and two are Christians more or less, and the four Houssas are with me in faith."

"And you?"

Abiboo, the Kano boy, smiled at Sanders' assumption of innocence.

"Lord," he said, "I follow the Prophet, believing only in the one God, beneficent and merciful."

"That is good," said Sanders. "Now let the men load wood, and Yoka shall have steam against moonrise, and all shall be ready for slipping."

At ten o'clock by his watch he fell-in his four Houssas, serving out to each a short carbine and a bandoleer. Then the party went ashore.

The king in his patience sat in his hut, and Sanders found him.

"You will stay here, Milini," he commanded, "and no blame shall come to you for anything that may happen this night."

"What will happen, master?"

"Who knows!" said Sanders, philosophically.

The streets were in pitch darkness, but Abiboo, carrying a lantern, led the way. Only occasionally did the party pass a tenanted hut. Generally they saw by the dull glow of the log that smouldered in every habitation that it was empty. Once a sick woman called to them in passing. It was near her time, she said, and there was none to help her in the supreme moment of her agony.

"God help you, sister!" said Sanders, ever in awe of the mysteries of birth. "I will send women to you. What is your name?"

"They will not come," said the plaintive voice. "To-night the men go out to war, and the women wait for the great dance."

"To-night?"

"To-night, master—so the ghosts of brass decree."

Sanders made a clicking noise with his mouth.

"That we shall see," he said, and went on.

The party reached the outskirts of the city. Before them, outlined against a bronze sky, was the dark bulk of a little hill, and this they skirted.

The bronze became red, and rose, and dull bronze again, as the fires that gave it colour leapt or fell. Turning the shoulder of the hill, Sanders had a full view of the scene.

Between the edge of the forest and slope of the hill was a broad strip of level land. On the left was the river, on the right was swamp and forest again.

In the very centre of the plain a huge fire burnt. Before it, supported by its poles, on two high trestles, a square box.

But the people!

A huge circle, squatting on its haunches, motionless, silent; men, women, children, tiny babies, at their mothers' hips they stretched; a solid wheel of humanity, with the box and the fire as a hub.

There was a lane through which a man might reach the box—a lane along which passed a procession of naked men, going and returning. These were they who replenished the fire, and Sanders saw them dragging fuel for that purpose. Keeping to the edge of the crowd, he worked his way to the opening. Then he looked round at his men.

"It is written," he said, in the curious Arabic of the Kano people, "that we shall carry away this false god. As to which of us shall live or die through this adventure, that is with Allah, who knows all things."

Then he stepped boldly along the lane. He had changed his white ducks for a dark blue uniform suit, and he was not observed by the majority until he came with his Houssas to the box. The heat from the fire was terrific, overpowering. Close at hand he saw that the fierceness of the blaze had warped the rough-hewn boards of the box, and through the opening he saw in the light a slab of stone.

"Take up the box quickly," he commanded, and the Houssas lifted the poles to their shoulders. Until then the great assembly had sat in silent wonder, but as the soldiers lifted their burden, a yell of rage burst from five thousand throats, and men leapt to their feet.

Sanders stood before the fire, one hand raised, and silence fell, curiosity dominating resentment.

"People of the Isisi," said Sanders, "let no man move until the god-stone has passed, for death comes quickly to those who cross the path of gods."

He had an automatic pistol in each hand, and the particular deity he was thinking of at the moment was not the one in the box.

The people hesitated, surging and swaying, as a mob will sway in its uncertainty.

With quick steps the bearers carried their burden through the lane; they had almost passed unmolested when an old woman shuffled forward and clutched at Sanders' arm.

"Lord, lord!" she quavered, "what will you do with our god?"

"Take him to the proper place," said Sanders, "being by Government appointed his keeper."

"Give me a sign," she croaked, and the people in her vicinity repeated, "A sign, master!"

"This is a sign," said Sanders, remembering the woman in labour. "By the god's favour there shall be born to Ifabi, wife of Adako, a male child."

He heard the babble of talk; he heard his message repeated over the heads of the crowd; he saw a party of women go scurrying back to the village; then he gave the order to march. There were murmurings, and once he heard a deep-voiced man begin the war-chant, but nobody joined him. Somebody—probably the same man—clashed his spear against his wicker shield, but his warlike example was not followed. Sanders gained the village street. Around him was such a press of people that he followed the swaying box with difficulty. The river was in sight; the moon, rising a dull, golden ball over the trees, laced the water with silver, and then there came a scream of rage.

"He lies! He lies! Ifabi, the wife of Adako, has a female child."

Sanders turned swiftly like a dog at bay; his lips upcurled in a snarl, his white, regular teeth showing.

"Now," said Sanders, speaking very quickly, "let any man raise his spear, and he dies."

Again they stood irresolute, and Sanders, over his shoulder, gave an order.

For a moment only the people hesitated; then, as the soldiers gripped the poles of the god-box, with one fierce yell they sprang forward.

A voice screamed something; and, as if by magic, the tumult ceased, and the crowd darted backward and outward, falling over one another in their frantic desire to escape.

Sanders, his pistol still loaded, stood in open-mouthed astonishment at the stampede.

Save for his men he was alone; and then he saw.

Along the centre of the street two men were walking. They were clad alike in short crimson kilts that left their knees bare; great brass helmets topped their heads, and brass cuirasses covered their breasts.

Sanders watched them as they came nearer, then: "If this is not fever, it is madness," he muttered, for what he saw were two Roman centurions, their heavy swords girt about their waists.

He stood still, and they passed him, so close that he saw on the boss of one shield the rough-moulded letters:—

"AUGUSTUS CAE."

"Fever" said Sanders emphatically, and followed the box to the ship.

When the steamer reached Lukati, Sanders was still in a condition of doubt, for his temperature was normal, and neither fever nor sun could be held accountable for the vision. Added to which, his men had seen the same thing.

He found the reinforcements his pigeon had brought, but they were unnecessary now.

"It beats me," he confessed to Carter, telling the story; "but we'll get out the stone; it might furnish an explanation. Centurions—bah!"

The stone, exposed in the light of day, was of greyish granite, such as Sanders did not remember having seen before.

"Here are the 'devil marks,'" he said, as he turned it over. "Possibly—whew!"

No wonder he whistled, for closely set were a number of printed characters; and Carter, blowing the dust, saw—

"MARIUS ET AUGUSTUS
CENT . . . . NERO
IMPERAT . . . . . IN DEUS
. . . . . DULCE."

That night, with great labour, Sanders, furbishing his rusty Latin, and filling in gaps, made a translation:

"Marius and Augustus,
Centurions of Nero, Cæsar and
Emperor,
Sleep sweetly with the gods."

"We are they who came beyond the wild lands which Hanno, the Carthaginian, found . . .

"Marcus Septimus went up into Egypt, and with him Decimus Superbus, but by the will of Cæsar, and the favour of the gods, we sailed to the black seas beyond. . . . . Here we lived, our ships suffering wreck, being worshipped by the barbarians, teaching them warlike practices.

. . . "You who come after . . . bear greetings to Rome to Cato Hippocritus, who dwells by the gate . . ."

27

Sanders shook his head when he had finished reading, and said it was "rum."

CHAPTER III.
BOSAMBO OF MONROVIA.

For many years have the Ochori people formed a sort of grim comic relief to the tragedy of African colonisation. Now it may well be that we shall laugh at the Ochori no more. Nor, in the small hours of the night, when conversation flags in the little circle about the fires in fishing camps, shall the sleepy-eyed be roused to merriment by stories of Ochori meekness. All this has come about by favour of the Liberian Government, though at present the Liberian Government is not aware of the fact.

With all due respect to the Republic of Liberia, I say that the Monrovians are naturally liars and thieves.

Once upon a time, that dignity might be added to the State, a warship was acquired—if I remember aright it was presented by a disinterested shipowner. The Government appointed three admirals, fourteen captains, and as many officers as the ship would hold, and they all wore gorgeous but ill-fitting uniforms. The Government would have appointed a crew also, but for the fact that the ship was not big enough to hold any larger number of people than its officers totalled.

This tiny man-of-war of the black republic went to sea once, the admirals and captains taking it in turn to stoke and steer—a very pleasing and novel sensation, this latter.

Coming back into the harbour, one of the admirals said—

"It is my turn to steer now," and took the wheel.

The ship struck a rock at the entrance of the harbour and went down. The officers escaped easily enough, for your Monrovian swims like a fish, but their uniforms were spoilt by the sea water. To the suggestion that salvage operations should be attempted to refloat the warship, the Government very wisely said no, they thought not.

"We know where she is," said the President—he was sitting on the edge of his desk at Government House, eating sardines with his fingers—"and if we ever want her, it will be comforting to know she is so close to us."

Nothing more would have been done in the matter but for the fact that the British Admiralty decided that the wreck was a danger to shipping, and issued orders forthwith for the place where it lay to be buoyed.

The Liberian Government demurred on account of expense, but on pressure being applied (I suspect the captain of H.M.S. *Dwarf*, who was a man with a bitter tongue) they agreed, and the bell-buoy was anchored to the submerged steamer.

It made a nice rowdy, clanging noise, did that bell, and the people of Monrovia felt they were getting their money's worth.

But all Monrovia is not made up of the freed American slaves who were settled there in 1821. There are people who are described in a lordly fashion by the true Monrovians as "indigenous natives," and the chief of these are the Kroomen, who pay no taxes, defy the Government, and at intervals tweak the official nose of the Republic.

The second day after the bell was in place, Monrovia awoke to find a complete silence reigning in the bay, and that in spite of a heavy swell. The bell was still, and two ex-admirals, who were selling fish on the foreshore, borrowed a boat and rowed out to investigate. The explanation was simple—the bell had been stolen.

"Now!" said the President of the Liberian Republic in despair, "may Beelzebub, who is the father and author of all sin, descend upon these thieving Kroomen!"

Another bell was attached. The same night it was stolen. Yet another bell was put to the buoy, and a boat-load of admirals kept watch. Throughout the night they sat, rising and falling with the swell, and the monotonous "clang-jangle-clong" was music in their ears. All night it sounded, but in the early morning, at the dark hour before the sun comes up, it seemed that the bell, still tolling, grew fainter and fainter.

"Brothers," said an admiral, "we are drifting away from the bell."

But the explanation was that the bell had drifted away from them, for, tired of half measures, the Kroomen had come and taken the buoy, bell and all, and to this day there is no mark to show where a sometime man-of-war rots in the harbour of Monrovia.

The ingenious soul who planned and carried out this theft was one Bosambo, who had three wives, one of whom, being by birth Congolaise, and untrustworthy, informed the police, and with some ceremony Bosambo was arrested and tried at the Supreme Court, where he was found guilty of "theft and high treason" and sentenced to ten years' penal servitude.

They took Bosambo back to prison, and Bosambo interviewed the black gaoler.

"My friend," he said, "I have a big ju-ju in the forest, and if you do not release me at once you and your wife shall die in great torment."

"Of your ju-ju I know nothing," said the gaoler philosophically, "but I receive two dollars a week for guarding prisoners, and if I let you escape I shall lose my job."

"I know a place where there is much silver hidden," said Bosambo with promptitude. "You and I will go to this place, and we shall be rich."

"If you knew where there was silver, why did you steal bells, which are of brass and of no particular value?" asked his unimaginative guard.

"I see that you have a heart of stone," said Bosambo, and went away to the forest settlement to chop down trees for the good of the State.

Four months after this, Sanders, Chief Commissioner for the Isisi, Ikeli, and Akasava countries, received, *inter alia*, a communication of a stereotyped description—

TO WHOM IT MAY CONCERN.

WANTED,—on a warrant issued by H.E. the President of Liberia, Bosambo Krooboy, who escaped from the penal settlement near Monrovia, after killing a guard. He is believed to be making for your country.

A description followed.

Sanders put the document away with other such notices—they were not infrequent in their occurrence—and gave his mind to the eternal problem of the Ochori.

Now, as ever, the Ochori people were in sad trouble. There is no other tribe in the whole of Africa that is as defenceless as the poor Ochori. The Fingoes, slaves as they are by name and tradition, were ferocious as the Masai, compared with the Ochori.

Sanders was a little impatient, and a deputation of three, who had journeyed down to headquarters to lay the grievances of the people before him, found him unsympathetic.

He interviewed them on his verandah.

"Master, no man leaves us in peace," said one. "Isisi folk, N'Gombi people from far-away countries, they come to us demanding this and that, and we give, being afraid."

"Afraid of what?" asked Sanders wearily.

"We fear death and pain, also burning and the taking of our women," said the other.

"Who is chief of you?" asked Sanders, wilfully ignorant.

"I am chief lord," said an elderly man, clad in a leopard skin.

"Go back to your people, chief, if indeed chief you are, and not some old woman without shame; go back and bear with you a fetish—a most powerful fetish—which shall be, as me, watching your interest and protecting you. This fetish you shall plant on the edge of your village that faces the sun at noon. You shall mark the place where it shall be planted, and at midnight, with proper ceremony, and the sacrifice of a young goat, you shall set my fetish in its place. And after that whosoever ill-treats you or robs you shall do so at some risk."

Sanders said this very solemnly, and the men of the deputation were duly impressed. More impressed were they when, before starting on their homeward journey, Sanders placed in their hands a stout pole, to the end of which was attached a flat board inscribed with certain marks.

They carried their trophy six days' journey through the forest, then four days' journey by canoe along the Little River, until they came to Ochori. There, by the light of the moon, with the sacrifice of two goats (to make sure), the pole was planted so that the board inscribed with mystic characters would face the sun at noon.

News travels fast in the back lands, and it came to the villages throughout the Isisi and the Akasava country that the Ochori were particularly protected by white magic. Protected they had always been, and many men had died at the white man's hand because the temptation to kill the Ochori folk had proved irresistible.

"I do not believe that Sandi has done this thing," said the chief of the Akasava. "Let us go across the river and see with our own eyes, and if they have lied we shall beat them with sticks, though let no man kill, because of Sandi and his cruelty."

So across the water they went, and marched until they came within sight of the Ochori city, and the Ochori people, hearing that the Akasava people were coming, ran away into the woods and hid, in accordance with their custom.

The Akasava advanced until they came to the pole stuck in the ground and the board with the devil marks.

Before this they stood in silence and in awe, and having made obeisance to it and sacrificed a chicken (which was the lawful property of the Ochori) they turned back.

After this came a party from Isisi, and they must needs come through the Akasava country.

They brought presents with them and lodged with the Akasava for one night.

"What story is this of the Ochori?" asked the Isisi chief in command; so the chief of the Akasava told him.

"You may save yourself the journey, for we have seen it."

"That," said the Isisi chief, "I will believe when I have seen."

"That is bad talk," said the Akasava people, who were gathered at the palaver; "these dogs of Isisi call us liars."

Nevertheless there was no bloodshed, and in the morning the Isisi went on their way.

The Ochori saw them coming, and hid in the woods, but the precaution was unnecessary, for the Isisi departed as they came.

Other folk made a pilgrimage to the Ochori, N'Gombi, Bokeli, and the Little People of the Forest, who were so shy that they came by night, and the Ochori people began to realise a sense of their importance.

Then Bosambo, a Krooman and an adventurer at large, appeared on the scene, having crossed eight hundred miles of wild land in the earnest hope that time would dull the memory of the Liberian Government and incidentally bring him to a land of milk and honey.

Now Bosambo had in his life been many things. He had been steward on an Elder Dempster boat, he had been scholar at a mission school—he was the proud possessor of a bound copy of *The Lives of the Saints*, a reward of industry—and among his accomplishments was a knowledge of English.

The hospitable Ochori received him kindly, fed him with sweet manioc and sugar-cane, and told him about Sandi's magic. After he had eaten, Bosambo walked down to the post and read the inscription—

TRESPASSERS BEWARE.

He was not impressed, and strolled back again thinking deeply.

"This magic," he said to the chief, "is good magic. I know, because I have white man's blood in my veins."

In support of this statement he proceeded to libel a perfectly innocent British official at Sierra Leone.

The Ochori were profoundly moved. They poured forth the story of their persecutions, a story which began in remote ages, when Tiganobeni, the great king, came down from the north and wasted the country as far south as the Isisi.

Bosambo listened—it took two nights and the greater part of a day to tell the story, because the official story-teller of the Ochori had only one method of telling—and when it was finished Bosambo said to himself—

"This is the people I have long sought. I will stay here."

Aloud he asked:

"How often does Sandi come to you?"

"Once every year, master," said the chief, "on the twelfth moon, and a little after."

"When came he last?"

"When this present moon is at full, three moons since; he comes after the big rains."

"Then," said Bosambo, again to himself, "for nine months I am safe."

They built him a hut and planted for him a banana grove and gave him seed. Then he demanded for wife the daughter of the chief, and although he offered nothing in payment the girl came to him. That a stranger lived in the chief village of the Ochori was remarked by the other tribes, for news of this kind spreads, but since he was married, and into the chief's family at that, it was accepted that the man must be of the Ochori folk, and such was the story that came to headquarters. Then the chief of the Ochori died. He died suddenly in some pain; but such deaths are common, and his son ruled in his place. Then the son died after the briefest reign, and Bosambo called the people together, the elders, the wise men, and the headmen of the country.

"It appears," he said, "that the many gods of the Ochori are displeased with you, and it has been revealed to me in a dream that I shall be chief of the Ochori. Therefore, O chiefs and wise men and headmen, bow before me, as is the custom, and I will make you a great people."

33

It is characteristic of the Ochori that no man said "nay" to him, even though in the assembly were three men who by custom might claim the chieftainship.

Sanders heard of the new chief and was puzzled.

"Etabo?" he repeated—this was how Bosambo called himself—"I do not remember the man—yet if he can put backbone into the people I do not care who he is."

Backbone or cunning, or both, Bosambo was certainly installed.

"He has many strange practices," reported a native agent to Sanders. "Every day he assembles the men of the village and causes them to walk past a *pelebi* (table) on which are many eggs. And it is his command that each man as he passes shall take an egg so swiftly that no eye may see him take it. And if the man bungle or break the egg, or be slow, this new chief puts shame upon him, whipping him."

"It is a game," said Sanders; but for the life of him he could not see what game it was. Report after report reached him of the new chief's madness. Sometimes he would take the unfortunate Ochori out by night, teaching them such things as they had never known before. Thus he instructed them in what manner they might seize upon a goat so that the goat could not cry. Also how to crawl on their bellies inch by inch so that they made no sound or sign. All these things the Ochori did, groaning aloud at the injustice and the labour of it.

"I'm dashed if I can understand it!" said Sanders, knitting his brows, when the last report came in. "With anybody but the Ochori this would mean war. But the Ochori!"

Notwithstanding his contempt for their fighting qualities, he kept his Police Houssas ready.

But there was no war. Instead, there came complaint from the Akasava that "many leopards were in the woods."

Leopards will keep, thought Sanders, and, anyway, the Akasava were good enough hunters to settle that palaver without outside help. The next report was alarming. In two weeks these leopards had carried off three score of goats, twenty bags of salt, and much ivory.

Leopards eat goats; there might conceivably be fastidious leopards that cannot eat goats without salt; but a leopard does not take ivory tusks even to pick his teeth with. So Sanders made haste to journey up the river, because little things were considerable in a country where people strain at gnats and swallow whole caravans.

"Lord, it is true," said the chief of the Akasava, with some emotion, "these goats disappear night by night, though we watch them; also the salt and ivory, because that we did not watch."

"But no leopard could take these things," said Sanders irritably. "These are thieves."

The chief's gesture was comprehensive.

"Who could thieve?" he said. "The N'Gombi people live very far away; also the Isisi. The Ochori are fools, and, moreover, afraid."

Then Sanders remembered the egg games, and the midnight manoeuvres of the Ochori.

"I will call on this new chief," he said; and crossed the river that day.

Sending a messenger to herald his coming, he waited two miles out of the city, and the councillors and wise men came out to him with offerings of fish and fruit.

"Where is your chief?" he asked.

"Lord, he is ill," they said gravely. "This day there came to him a feeling of sickness, and he fell down moaning. We have carried him to his hut."

Sanders nodded.

"I will see him," he said grimly.

They led him to the door of the chief's hut, and Sanders went in. It was very dark, and in the darkest corner lay a prostrate man. Sanders bent over him, touched his pulse lightly, felt gingerly for the swelling on the neck behind the ears for a sign of sleeping sickness. No symptom could he find; but on the bare shoulder, as his fingers passed over the man's flesh, he felt a scar of singular regularity; then he found another, and traced their direction. The convict brand of the Monrovian Government was familiar to him.

"I thought so," said Sanders, and gave the moaning man a vigorous kick.

"Come out into the light, Bosambo of Monrovia," he said; and Bosambo rose obediently and followed the Commissioner into the light.

They stood looking at one another for several minutes; then Sanders, speaking in the dialect of the Pepper Coast, said—

"I have a mind to hang you, Bosambo."

"That is as your Excellency wishes," said Bosambo.

Sanders said nothing, tapping his boot with his walking-stick and gazing thoughtfully downward.

"Having made thieves, could you make men of these people?" he said, after a while.

"I think they could fight now, for they are puffed with pride because they have robbed the Akasava," said Bosambo.

Sanders bit the end of his stick like a man in doubt.

"There shall be neither theft nor murder," he said. "No more chiefs or chiefs' sons shall die suddenly," he added significantly.

"Master, it shall be as you desire."

"As for the goats you have stolen, them you may keep, and the teeth (ivory) and the salt also. For if you hand them back to Akasava you will fill their stomachs with rage, and that would mean war."

Bosambo nodded slowly.

"Then you shall remain, for I see you are a clever man, and the Ochori need such as you. But if——"

"Master, by the fat of my heart I will do as you wish," said Bosambo; "for I have always desired to be a chief under the British."

Sanders was half-way back to headquarters before he missed his field-glasses, and wondered where he could have dropped them. At that identical moment Bosambo was exhibiting the binoculars to his admiring people.

"From this day forth," said Bosambo, "there shall be no lifting of goats nor stealing of any kind. This much I told the great Sandi, and as a sign of his love, behold, he gave me these things of magic that eat up space."

"Lord," said a councillor in awe, "did you know the Great One?"

"I have cause to know him," said Bosambo modestly, "for I am his son."

Fortunately Sanders knew nothing of this interesting disclosure.

CHAPTER IV.
THE DROWSY ONE.

There were occasions when Sanders came up against the outer world, when he learnt, with something like bewilderment, that beyond the farthermost forests, beyond the lazy, swelling, blue sea, there were men and women who lived in houses and carefully tabooed such subjects as violent death and such horrid happenings as were daily features of his life.

He had to treat with folk who, in the main, were illogical and who believed in spirits. When you deal in the abstract with government of races so influenced, a knowledge of constitutional law and economics is fairly valueless.

There is one type of man that can rule native provinces wisely, and that type is best represented by Sanders.

There are other types, as, for instance:

Once upon a time a young man came from England with a reputation. He was sent by the Colonial Office to hold a district under Sanders as Deputy Commissioner. He was a Bachelor of Law, had read Science, and had acquired in a methodical fashion a working acquaintance with Swaheli, bacteriology, and medicines. He was a very grave young man, and the first night of his arrival he kept Sanders (furtively yawning) out of his bed whilst he demonstrated a system whereby the aboriginal could be converted—not converted spiritually, but from unproductive vagrancy to a condition of good citizenship.

Sanders said nothing beyond using the conventional expressions of polite interest, and despatched the young man and his tremendous baggage to an up-country station, with his official blessing.

Torrington—this was the grave young man's name—established himself at Entoli, and started forth to instil into the heathen mind the elementary principles of applied mechanics. In other words he taught them, through the medium of Swaheli—which they imperfectly understood—and a tin kettle, the lesson of steam. They understood the kettle part, but could not quite comprehend what meat he was cooking, and when he explained for the fortieth time that he was only cooking water, they glanced significantly one at the other and agreed that he was not quite right in his head.

They did not tell him this much to his face, for cannibals have very good manners—though their table code leaves much to be desired.

Mr. Torrington tried them with chemical experiments, showing them how sulphuric acid applied to sugar produced Su^2, Su^4, or words to that effect. He gained a reputation as a magician as a result, and in more huts than one he was regarded and worshipped as a Great and Clever Devil—which in a sense he was. But the first time he came up against the spirit of the people, his science, his law, and his cut-and-dried theories went *phutt*! And that is where Sanders came in—Sanders who had forgotten all the chemistry he ever knew, and who, as a student of Constitutional Law, was the rankest of failures.

It came about in this way.

There was a young man in Isisi who prophesied that on such a day, at such an hour, the river would rise and drown the people. When Mr. Torrington heard of this prophecy he was amused, and at first took no notice of it. But it occurred to him that here might be a splendid opportunity for revealing to the barbarian a little of that science with which he was so plentifully endowed.

So he drew a large sectional plan, showing—

(*a*) the bed of the river;
(*b*) the height of the banks;
(*c*) the maximum rise of the river;
(*d*) the height of the surrounding country; and demonstrated as plainly as possible the utter absurdity of the prophecy.

Yet the people were unconvinced, and were preparing to abandon the village when Sanders arrived on the scene. He sent for the prophet, who was a young man of neurotic tendencies, and had a wooden prison cage built on the bank of the river, into which the youth was introduced.

"You will stay here," said Sanders, "and when the river rises you must prophesy that it will fall again, else assuredly you will be drowned."

Whereupon the people settled down again in their homes and waited for the river to drown the prophet and prove his words. But the river at this season of the year was steadily falling, and the prophet, like many another, was without honour in his own country.

Sanders went away; and, although somewhat discouraged, Mr. Torrington resumed his experiments. First of all, he took up sleeping sickness, and put in three months' futile work, impressing nobody save a gentleman of whom more must be written in a further chapter. Then he dropped that study suddenly and went to another.

He had ideas concerning vaccination, but the first baby he vaccinated died of croup, and Torrington came flying down the river telling Sanders a rambling story of a populace infuriated and demanding his blood. Then Torrington went home.

"The country is now quiet," wrote Sanders to the Administrator, with sardonic humour. "There are numerous palavers pending, but none of any particular moment. The Isisi people are unusually quiet, and Bosambo, the Monrovian, of whom I have written your Excellency, makes a model chief for the Ochori. No thefts have been traced to him for three months. I should be grateful if full information could be supplied to me concerning an expedition which at the moment is traversing this country under the style of the Isisi Exploitation Syndicate."

Curiously enough, Torrington had forgotten the fact that a member of this expedition had been one of the most interested students of his sleeping sickness clinics.

The Isisi Exploitation Syndicate, Limited, was born between the entrée and the sweet at the house of a gentleman whose Christian name was Isidore, and who lived in Maida Vale. At dinner one night with a dear friend—who called himself McPherson every day of the year except on Yum Kippur, when he frankly admitted that he had been born Isaacs—the question of good company titles came up, and Mr. McPherson said he had had the "Isisi Exploitation" in his mind for many years. With the aid of an atlas the Isisi country was discovered. It was one of those atlases on which are inscribed the staple products of the lands, and across the Isisi was writ fair "Rubber," "Kola-nut," "Mahogany," and "Tobacco."

I would ask the reader to particularly remember "Tobacco."

"There's a chief I've had some correspondence with," said Mr. McPherson, chewing his cigar meditatively; "we could get a sort of concession from him. It would have to be done on the quiet, because the country is a British Protectorate. Now, if we could get a man who'd put up the stuff, and send him out to fix the concession, we'd have a company floated before you could say knife."

Judicious inquiry discovered the man in Claude Hyall Cuthbert, a plutocratic young gentleman, who, on the strength of once having nearly shot a lion in Uganda, was accepted by a large circle of acquaintances as an authority on Africa.

Cuthbert, who dabbled in stocks and shares, was an acquisition to any syndicate, and on the understanding that part of his duty would be the obtaining of the concession, he gladly financed the syndicate to the extent of seven thousand pounds, four thousand of which Messrs. Isidore and McPherson very kindly returned to him to cover the cost of his expedition.

The other three thousand were earmarked for office expenses.

As Mr. McPherson truly said:

"Whatever happens, we're on velvet, my boy," which was perfectly true.

Before Cuthbert sailed, McPherson offered him a little advice.

"Whatever you do," he said, "steer clear of that dam' Commissioner Sanders. He's one of those pryin', interferin'——"

"I know the breed," said Cuthbert wisely. "This is not my first visit to Africa. Did I ever tell you about the lion I shot in Uganda?"

A week later he sailed.

In course of time came a strange white man through Sanders' domain. This white man, who was Cuthbert, was following the green path to death—but this he did not know. He threw his face to the forest, as the natives say, and laughed, and the people of the village of O'Tembi, standing before their wattle huts, watched him in silent wonder.

It was a wide path between huge trees, and the green of the undergrowth was flecked with sunlight, and, indeed, the green path was beautiful to the eye, being not unlike a parkland avenue.

N'Beki, chief of this village of the O'Tembi, a very good old man, went out to the path when the white man began his journey.

"White man," he said solemnly, "this is the road to hell, where all manner of devils live. Night brings remorse, and dawn brings self-hatred, which is worse than death."

Cuthbert, whose Swaheli was faulty, and whose Bomongo talk was nil, grinned impatiently as his coastboy translated unpicturesquely.

"Dam nigger done say, this be bad place, no good; he say bimeby you libe for die."

"Tell him to go to blazes!" said Cuthbert noisily; "and, look here, Flagstaff, ask him where the rubber is, see? Tell him we know all about the forest, and ask him about the elephants, where their playground is?"

Cuthbert was broad-shouldered and heavily built, and under his broad sun-helmet his face was very hot and moist.

"Tell the white man," said the chief quietly, "there is no rubber within seven days' journey, and that we do not know ivory; elephants there were *cala cala*—but not now."

"He's a liar!" was Cuthbert's only comment. "Get these beggars moving, Flagstaff. Hi, *alapa', avanti, trek!*"

"These beggars," a straggling line of them, resumed their loads uncomplainingly. They were good carriers, as carriers go, and only two had died since the march began.

Cuthbert stood and watched them pass, using his stick dispassionately upon the laggards. Then he turned to go.

"Ask him," he said finally, "why he calls this the road to what-d'ye-call-it?"

The old man shook his head.

"Because of the devils," he said simply.

"Tell him he's a silly ass!" bellowed Cuthbert and followed his carriers.

This natural path the caravan took extended in almost a straight line through the forest. It was a strange path because of its very smoothness, and the only drawback lay in the fact that it seemed to be the breeding-place of flies—little black flies, as big as the house-fly of familiar shape, if anything a little bigger.

They terrified the natives for many reasons, but principally because they stung. They did not terrify Cuthbert, because he was dressed in tapai cloth; none the less, there were times when these black flies found joints in his armour and roused him to anger. This path extended ten miles and made pleasant travelling. Then the explorer struck off into the forest, following another path, well beaten, but more difficult.

By devious routes Mr. Cuthbert came into the heart of Sanders' territories, and he was successful in this, that he avoided Sanders. He had with him a caravan of sixty men and an interpreter, and in due course he reached his objective, which was the village of a great chief ruling a remarkable province—Bosambo, of the Ochori, no less; sometime Krooman, steward of the Elder Dempster line, chief on sufferance, but none the less an interesting person. Bosambo, you may be sure, came out to greet his visitor.

"Say to him," said Cuthbert to his interpreter, "that I am proud to meet the great chief."

"Lord chief," said the interpreter in the vernacular, "this white man is a fool, and has much money."

"So I see," said Bosambo.

"Tell him," said Cuthbert, with all the dignity of an ambassador, "that I have come to bring him wonderful presents."

"The white man says," said the interpreter, "that if he is sure you are a good man he will give you presents. Now," said the interpreter carefully, "as I am the only man who can speak for you, let us make arrangements. You shall give me one-third of all he offers. Then will I persuade him to continue giving, since he is the father of mad people."

"And you," said Bosambo briefly, "are the father of liars."

He made a sign to his guard, and they seized upon the unfortunate interpreter and led him forth. Cuthbert, in a sweat of fear, pulled a revolver.

"Master," said Bosambo loftily, "you no make um fuss. Dis dam' nigger, he no good; he make you speak bad t'ings. I speak um English proper. You sit down, we talk um."

So Cuthbert sat down in the village of Ochori, and for three days there was a great giving of presents, and signing of concessions. Bosambo conceded the Ochori country—that was a small thing. He granted forest rights of the Isisi, he sold the Akasava, he bartered away the Lulungo territories and the "native products thereof"—I quote from the written document now preserved at the Colonial Office and bearing the scrawled signature of Bosambo—and he added, as a lordly afterthought, the Ikeli district.

"What about river rights?" asked the delighted Cuthbert.

"What will you give um?" demanded Bosambo cautiously.

"Forty English pounds?" suggested Cuthbert.

"I take um," said Bosambo.

It was a remarkably simple business; a more knowledgeable man than Cuthbert would have been scared by the easiness of his success, but Cuthbert was too satisfied with himself to be scared at anything.

It is said that his leave-taking with Bosambo was of an affecting character, that Bosambo wept and embraced his benefactor's feet.

Be that as it may, his "concessions" in his pocket, Cuthbert began his coastward journey, still avoiding Sanders.

He came to Etebi and found a deputy-commissioner, who received him with open arms. Here Cuthbert stayed a week.

Mr. Torrington at the time was tremendously busy with a scheme for stamping out sleeping sickness. Until then, Cuthbert was under the impression that it was a pleasant disease, the principal symptom of which was a painless coma. Fascinated, he extended his stay to a fortnight, seeing many dreadful sights, for Torrington had established a sort of amateur clinic, and a hundred cases a day came to him for treatment.

"And it comes from the bite of a tsetse fly?" said Cuthbert. "Show me a tsetse."

Torrington obliged him, and when the other saw the little black insect he went white to the lips.

"My God!" he whispered, "I've been bitten by that!"

"It doesn't follow——" began Torrington; but Cuthbert was blundering and stumbling in wild fear to his carriers' camp.

"Get your loads!" he yelled. "Out of this cursed country we get as quick as we can!"

Torrington, with philosophical calm, endeavoured to reassure him, but he was not to be appeased.

He left Etebi that night and camped in the forest. Three days later he reached a mission station, where he complained of headaches and pains in the neck (he had not attended Torrington's clinics in vain). The missionary, judging from the man's haggard appearance and general incoherence that he had an attack of malaria, advised him to rest for a few days; but Cuthbert was all a-fret to reach the coast. Twenty miles from the mission, Cuthbert sent his carriers back, and said he would cover the last hundred miles of the journey alone.

To this extraordinary proposition the natives agree—from that day Cuthbert disappeared from the sight of man.

Sanders was taking a short cut through the forest to avoid the interminable twists and bends of the river, when he came suddenly upon a village of death—four sad little huts, built hastily amidst a tangle of underwood. He called, but nobody answered him. He was too wary to enter any of the crazy habitations.

He knew these little villages in the forest. It was the native custom to take the aged and the dying—especially those who died sleepily—to far-away places, beyond the reach of man, and leave them there with a week's food and a fire, to die in decent solitude.

He called again, but only the forest answered him. The chattering, noisy forest, all a-crackle with the movements of hidden things. Yet there was a fire burning which told of life.

Sanders resumed his journey, first causing a quantity of food to be laid in a conspicuous place for the man who made the fire.

He was on his way to take evidence concerning the disappearance of Cuthbert. It was the fourth journey of its kind he had attempted. There had been palavers innumerable.

Bosambo, chief of the Ochori, had sorrowfully disgorged the presents he had received, and admitted his fault.

"Lord!" he confessed, "when I was with the white man on the coast I learnt the trick of writing—it is a cursed gift—else all this trouble would not have come about. For, desiring to show my people how great a man I was, I wrote a letter in the English fashion, and sent it by messenger to the coast and thence to friends in Sierra Leone, telling them of my fortune. Thus the people in London came to know of the treasure of this land."

Sanders, in a few illuminative sentences, conveyed his impression of Bosambo's genius.

"You slave and son of a slave," he said, "whom I took from a prison to rule the Ochori, why did you deceive this white man, selling him lands that were not yours?"

"Lord!" said Bosambo simply, "there was nothing else I could sell."

But there was no clue here as to Cuthbert's whereabouts, nor at the mission station, nor amongst the carriers detained on suspicion. One man might have thrown light upon the situation, but Torrington was at home fulfilling the post of assistant examiner in mechanics at South Kensington (more in his element there) and filling in his spare time with lecturing on "The Migration of the Bantu Races."

So that the end of Sanders' fourth quest was no more successful than the third, or the second, or the first, and he retraced his steps to headquarters, feeling somewhat depressed.

He took the path he had previously traversed, and came upon the Death Camp late in the afternoon. The fire still burnt, but the food he had placed had disappeared. He hailed the hut in the native tongue, but no one answered him. He waited for a little while, and then gave orders for more food to be placed on the ground.

"Poor devil!" said Sanders, and gave the order to march. He himself had taken half a dozen steps, when he stopped. At his feet something glittered in the fading light. He stooped and picked it up. It was an exploded cartridge. He examined it carefully, smelt it—it had been recently fired. Then he found another. They were Lee-Metford, and bore the mark "'07," which meant that they were less than a year old.

He was still standing with the little brass cylinders in his hand, when Abiboo came to him.

"Master," said the Houssa, "who ties monkeys to trees with ropes?"

"Is that a riddle?" asked Sanders testily, for his mind was busy on this matter of cartridges.

Abiboo for answer beckoned him.

Fifty yards from the hut was a tree, at the foot of which, whimpering and chattering and in a condition of abject terror, were two small black monkeys tethered by ropes.

They spat and grinned ferociously as Sanders approached them. He looked from the cartridges to the monkeys and back to the cartridges again, then he began searching the grass. He found two more empty shells and a rusting lancet, such as may be found in the pocket-case of any explorer.

Then he walked back to the hut before which the fire burnt, and called softly—

"Mr. Cuthbert!"

There was no answer, and Sanders called again—

"Mr. Cuthbert!"

From the interior of the hut came a groan.

"Leave me alone. I have come here to die!" said a muffled voice.

"Come out and be civil," said Sanders coolly; "you can die afterwards."

After a few moments' delay there issued from the door of the hut the wreck of a man, with long hair and a month-old beard, who stood sulkily before the Commissioner.

"Might I ask," said Sanders, "what your little game is?"

The other shook his head wearily. He was a pitiable sight. His clothes were in tatters; he was unwashed and grimy.

"Sleeping sickness," he said wearily. "Felt it coming on—seen what horrible thing it was—didn't want to be a burden. Oh, my God! What a fool I've been to come to this filthy country!"

"That's very likely," said Sanders. "But who told you that you had sleeping sickness?"

"Know it—know it," said the listless man.

"Sit down," said Sanders. The other obeyed, and Sanders applied the superficial tests.

"If you've got sleeping sickness," said Sanders, after the examination, "I'm suffering from religious mania—man, you're crazy!"

Yet there was something in Cuthbert's expression that was puzzling. He was dull, heavy, and stupid. His movements were slow and lethargic.

Sanders watched him as he pulled a black wooden pipe from his ragged pocket, and with painful slowness charged it from a skin pouch.

"It's got me, I tell you," muttered Cuthbert, and lit the pipe with a blazing twig from the fire. "I knew it (puff) as soon as that fellow Torrington (puff) described the symptoms (puff);—felt dull and sleepy—got a couple of monkeys and injected my blood (puff)—*they* went drowsy, too—sure sign——"

"Where did you get that tobacco from?" demanded Sanders quickly.

Cuthbert took time to consider his answer.

"Fellow gave it me—chief fellow, Bosambo. Native tobacco, but not bad—he gave me a devil of a lot."

"So I should say," said Sanders, and reaching over took the pouch and put it in his pocket.

When Sanders had seen Mr. Cuthbert safe on board a homeward-bound steamer, he took his twenty Houssas to the Ochori country to arrest Bosambo, and expected Bosambo would fly; but the imperturbable chief awaited his coming, and offered him the customary honours.

"I admit I gave the white man the hemp," he said. "I myself smoke it, suffering no ill. How was I to know that it would make him sleep?"

"Why did you give it to him?" demanded Sanders.

Bosambo looked the Commissioner full in the face.

"Last moon you came, lord, asking why I gave him the Isisi country and the rights of the little river, because these were not mine to give. Now you come to me saying why did I give the white man native tobacco—Lord, that was the only thing I gave him that was mine."

CHAPTER V.
THE SPECIAL COMMISSIONER.

The Hon. George Tackle had the good fortune to be the son of his father; otherwise I am free to confess he had no claim to distinction. But his father, being the proprietor of the *Courier and Echo* (with which are incorporated I don't know how many dead and gone stars of the Fleet Street firmament), George had a "pull" which no amount of competitive merit could hope to contend with, and when the stories of atrocities in the district of Lukati began to leak out and questions were asked in Parliament, George opened his expensively-bound Gazetteer, discovered that the district of Lukati was in British territory, and instantly demanded that he should be sent out to investigate these crimes, which were a blot upon our boasted civilisation.

His father agreed, having altogether a false appreciation of his son's genius, and suggested that George should go to the office and "get all the facts" regarding the atrocities. George, with a good-natured smile of amusement at the bare thought of anybody instructing him in a subject on which he was so thoroughly conversant, promised; but the *Courier and Echo* office did not see him, and the librarian of the newspaper, who had prepared a really valuable dossier of newspaper cuttings, pamphlets, maps, and health hints for the young man's guidance, was dismayed to learn that the confident youth had sailed without any further instruction in the question than a man might secure from the hurried perusal of the scraps which from day to day appeared in the morning press.

As a special correspondent, I adduce, with ill-suppressed triumph, the case of the Hon. George Tackle as an awful warning to all newspaper proprietors who allow their parental affections to overcome their good judgment.

All that the Hon. George knew was that at Lukati there had been four well-authenticated cases of barbarous acts of cruelty against natives, and that the Commissioner of the district was responsible for the whippings and the torture. He thought, did the Hon. George, that this was all that it was necessary to know. But this is where he made his big mistake.

Up at Lukati all sorts of things happened, as Commissioner Sanders knows, to his cost. Once he visited the district and left it tranquil, and for Carter, his deputy, whom he left behind, the natives built a most beautiful hut, planting gardens about, all off their own bat.

One day, when Carter had just finished writing an enthusiastic report on the industry of his people, and the whole-hearted way they were taking up and supporting the new régime, the chief of the village, whom Carter had facetiously named O'Leary (his born name was indeed Olari), came to him.

Carter at the moment was walking through the well-swept street of the village with his hands in his coat pockets and his big white helmet tipped on the back of his head because the sun was setting at his back.

"Father," said the Chief Olari, "I have brought these people to see you."

He indicated with a wave of his hand six strange warriors carrying their shields and spears, who looked at him dispassionately.

Carter nodded.

"They desire," said Olari, "to see the wonderful little black fetish that my father carries in his pocket that they may tell their people of its powers."

"Tell your people," said Carter good-humouredly, "that I have not got the fetish with me—if they will come to my hut I will show them its wonders."

Whereupon Olari lifted his spear and struck at Carter, and the six warriors sprang forward together. Carter fought gamely, but he was unarmed.

When Sanders heard the news of his subordinate's death he did not faint or fall into a fit of insane cursing. He was sitting on his broad verandah at headquarters when the dusty messenger came. He rose with pursed lips and frowning eyes, fingering the letter—this came from Tollemache, inspector of police at Bokari—and paced the verandah.

"Poor chap, poor chap!" was all that he said.

He sent no message to Olari; he made no preparations for a punitive raid; he went on signing documents, inspecting Houssas, attending dinner parties, as though Carter had never lived or died. All these things the spies of Olari reported, and the chief was thankful.

Lukati being two hundred miles from headquarters, through a savage and mountainous country, an expedition was no light undertaking, and the British Government, rich as it is, cannot afford to spend a hundred thousand pounds to avenge the death of a subordinate official. Of this fact Sanders was well aware, so he employed his time in collecting and authenticating the names of Carter's assassins. When he had completed them he went a journey seventy miles into the bush to the great witch-doctor Kelebi, whose name was known throughout the coast country from Dakka to the Eastern borders of Togoland.

"Here are the names of men who have put shame upon me," he said; "but principally Olari, chief of the Lukati people."

"I will put a spell upon Olari," said the witch-doctor; "a very bad spell, and upon these men. The charge will be six English pounds."

Sanders paid the money, and "dashed" two bottles of square-face and a piece of proper cloth. Then he went back to headquarters.

One night through the village of Lukati ran a whisper, and the men muttered the news with fearful shivers and backward glances.

"Olari, the chief, is cursed!"

Olari heard the tidings from his women, and came out of his hut into the moonlight, raving horribly.

The next day he sickened, and on the fifth day he was near to dead and suffering terrible pains, as also were six men who helped in the slaying of Carter. That they did not die was no fault of the witch-doctor, who excused his failure on account of the great distance between himself and his subjects.

As for Sanders, he was satisfied, saying that even the pains were cheap at the price, and that it would give him great satisfaction to write "finis" to Olari with his own hand.

A week after this, Abiboo, Sanders' favourite servant, was taken ill. There was no evidence of fever or disease, only the man began to fade as it were.

Making inquiries, Sanders discovered that Abiboo had offended the witch-doctor Kelebi, and that the doctor had sent him the death message.

Sanders took fifty Houssas into the bush and interviewed the witch-doctor.

"I have reason," he said, "for believing you to be a failure as a slayer of men."

"Master," said Kelebi in extenuation, "my magic cannot cross mountains, otherwise Olari and his friends would have died."

"That is as it may be," said Sanders. "I am now concerned with magic nearer at hand, and I must tell you that the day after Abiboo dies I will hang you."

"Father," said Kelebi emphatically, "under those circumstances Abiboo shall live."

Sanders gave him a sovereign, and rode back to headquarters, to find his servant on the high road to recovery.

I give you this fragment of Sanders' history, because it will enable you to grasp the peculiar environment in which Sanders spent the greater part of his life, and because you will appreciate all the better the irony of the situation created by the coming of the Hon. George Tackle.

Sanders was taking breakfast on the verandah of his house. From where he sat he commanded across the flaming beauties of his garden a view of a broad, rolling, oily sea, a golden blaze of light under the hot sun. There was a steamer lying three miles out (only in five fathoms of water at that), and Sanders, through his glasses, recognised her as the Elder Dempster boat that brought the monthly mail. Since there were no letters on his table, and the boat had been "in" for two hours, he gathered that there was no mail for him, and was thankful, for he had outlived the sentimental period of life when letters were pleasant possibilities.

Having no letters, he expected no callers, and the spectacle of the Hon. George being carried in a hammock into his garden was astonishing.

The Hon. George carefully alighted, adjusted his white pith helmet, smoothed the creases from his immaculate ducks, and mounted the steps that led to the stoep.

"How do?" said the visitor. "My name is Tackle—George Tackle." He smiled, as though to say more was an insult to his hearer's intelligence.

Sanders bowed, a little ceremoniously for him. He felt that his visitor expected this.

"I'm out on a commission," the Hon. George went on. "As you've doubtless heard, my governor is the proprietor of the *Courier and Echo*, and so he thought I'd better go out and see the thing for myself. I've no doubt the whole thing is exaggerated——"

"Hold hard," said Sanders, a light dawning on him. "I gather that you are a sort of correspondent of a newspaper?"

"Exactly."

"That you have come to inquire into——"

"Treatment of natives, and all that," said the Hon. George easily.

"And what is wrong with the treatment of the native?" asked Sanders sweetly.

The hon. gentleman made an indefinite gesture.

"You know—things in newspapers—missionaries," he said rapidly, being somewhat embarrassed by the realisation that the man, if any, responsible for the outrages was standing before him.

"I never read the newspapers," said Sanders, "and——"

"Of course," interrupted the Hon. George eagerly, "we can make it all right as far as you are concerned."

"Oh, thank you!" Sanders' gratitude was a little overdone, but he held out his hand. "Well, I wish you luck—let me know how you get on."

The Hon. George Tackle was frankly nonplussed.

"But excuse me," he said, "where—how——Hang it all, where am I to put up?"

"Here?"

"Yes — dash it, my kit is on shore! I thought——"

"You thought I'd put you up?"

"Well, I did think——"

"That I'd fall on your neck and welcome you?"

"Not exactly, but——"

"Well," said Sanders, carefully folding his napkin, "I'm not so glad to see you as all that."

"I suppose not," said the Hon. George, bridling.

"Because you're a responsibility—I hate extra responsibility. You can pitch your tent just wherever you like—but I cannot offer you the hospitality you desire."

"I shall report this matter to the Administrator," said the Hon. George ominously.

"You may report it to my grandmother's maiden aunt," said Sanders politely.

Half an hour later he saw the Hon. George rejoin the ship that brought him to Isisi Bassam, and chuckled. George would go straight to the Administrator, and would receive a reception beside which a Sahara storm would be zephyrs of Araby.

At the same time Sanders was a little puzzled, and not a little hurt. There never had been a question of atrocities in his district, and he was puzzled to account for the rumours that had brought the "commissioner" on his tour of investigation—could it be a distorted account of Olari's punishment?

"Go quickly to the ship, taking a book to the lord who has just gone from here," was his command to a servant, and proceeded to scribble a note:—

"I am afraid," he wrote, "I was rather rude to you—not understanding what the devil you were driving at. An overwhelming curiosity directs me to invite you to share my bungalow until such time as you are ready to conduct your investigation."

The Hon. George read this with a self-satisfied smirk.

"The way to treat these fellows," he said to the Elder Dempster captain, "is to show 'em you'll stand no nonsense. I thought he'd climb down."

The Elder Dempster captain, who knew Sanders by repute, smiled discreetly, but said nothing. Once more the special correspondent's mountain of baggage was embarked in the surf boat, and the Hon. George waved a farewell to his friends on the steamer.

The Elder Dempster skipper, leaning over the side of his bridge, watched the surf boat rising and falling in the swell.

"There goes a man who's looking for trouble," he said, "and I wouldn't take a half-share of the trouble he's going to find for five hundred of the best. Is that blessed anchor up yet, Mr. Simmons? Half ahead—set her due west, Mr. What's-your-name."

It was something of a triumph for the Hon. George. There were ten uniformed policemen awaiting him on the smooth beach to handle his baggage, and Sanders came down to his garden gate to meet him.

"The fact of it is——" began Sanders awkwardly; but the magnanimous George raised his hand.

"Let bygones," he said, "be bygones."

Sanders was unaccountably annoyed by this generous display. Still more so was he when the correspondent refused to reopen the question of atrocities.

"As your guest," said George solemnly, "I feel that it would be better for all concerned if I pursued an independent investigation. I shall endeavour as far as possible, to put myself in your place, to consider all extenuating circumstances——"

"Oh, have a gin-swizzle!" said Sanders rudely and impatiently; "you make me tired."

"Look here," he said later, "I will only ask you two questions. Where are these atrocities supposed to have taken place?"

"In the district of Lukati," said the Hon. George.

"Olari," thought Sanders. "Who was the victim?" he asked.

"There were several," said the correspondent, and produced his note-book. "You understand that I'd really much rather not discuss the matter with you, but, since you insist," he read, "Efembi of Wastambo."

"Oh!" said Sanders, and his eyebrows rose

"Kabindo of Machembi."

"Oh, lord!" said Sanders.

The Hon. George read six other cases, and with every one a line was wiped from Sanders' forehead.

When the recital was finished the Commissioner said slowly—

"I can make a statement to you which will save you a great deal of unnecessary trouble."

"I would rather you didn't," said George, in his best judicial manner.

"Very good," said Sanders; and went away whistling to order dinner.

Over the meal he put it to the correspondent:

"There are a number of people on this station who are friends of mine. I won't disguise the fact from you—there is O'Neill, in charge of the Houssas; the doctor, Kennedy, the chap in charge of the survey party; and half a dozen more. Would you like to question them?"

"They are friends of yours?"

"Yes, personal friends."

"Then," said the Hon. George, gravely, "perhaps it would be better if I did not see them."

"As you wish," said Sanders.

With an escort of four Houssas, and fifty carriers recruited from the neighbouring villages, the Hon. George departed into the interior, and Sanders saw him off.

"I cannot, of course, guarantee your life," he said, at parting, "and I must warn you that the Government will not be responsible for any injury that comes to you."

"I understand," said the Hon. George knowingly, "but I am not to be deterred. I come from a stock——"

"I dare say," Sanders cut his genealogical reminiscences short; "but the last traveller who was 'chopped' in the bush was a D'Arcy, and his people came over with the Conqueror."

The correspondent took the straight path to Lukati, and at the end of the third day's march came to the village of Mfabo, where lived the great witch-doctor, Kelebi.

George pitched his camp outside the village, and, accompanied by his four Houssas, paid a call upon the chief, which was one of the first mistakes he made, for he should have sent for the chief to call upon him; and if he called upon anybody, he should have made his visit to the witch-doctor, who was a greater man than forty chiefs.

In course of time, however, he found himself squatting on the ground outside the doctor's house, engaged, through the medium of the interpreter he had brought from Sierra Leone, in an animated conversation with the celebrated person.

"Tell him," said George to his interpreter, "that I am a great white chief whose heart bleeds for the native."

"Is he a good man?" asked George.

The witch-doctor, with the recollection of Sanders' threat, said "No!"

"Why?" asked the Hon. George eagerly. "Does he beat the people?"

Not only did he beat the people, explained the witch-doctor with relish, but there were times when he burnt them alive.

"This is a serious charge," said George, wagging his head warningly; nevertheless he wrote with rapidity in his diary:——

"Interviewed Kelebi, respected native doctor, who states:

"'I have lived all my life in this district, and have never known so cruel a man as Sandi (Sanders). I remember once he caused a man to be drowned, the man's name I forget; on another occasion he burned a worthy native alive for refusing to guide him and his Houssas through the forest. I also remember the time when he put a village to the fire, causing the people great suffering.

"'The people of the country groan under his oppressions, for from time to time he comes demanding money and crops, and if he does not receive all that he asks for he flogs the villagers until they cry aloud.'"

(I rather suspect that there is truth in the latter statement, for Sanders finds no little difficulty in collecting the hut-tax, which is the Government's due.)

George shook his head when he finished writing.

"This," he said, "looks very bad."

He shook hands with the witch-doctor, and that aged villain looked surprised, and asked a question in the native tongue.

"You no be fit to dash him somet'ing," said the interpreter.

"Dash him?"

"Give 'um present—bottle gin."

"Certainly not," said George. "He may be satisfied with the knowledge that he is rendering a service to humanity; that he is helping the cause of a down-trodden people."

The witch-doctor said something in reply, which the interpreter very wisely refrained from putting into English.

"How go the investigations?" asked the captain of Houssas three weeks later.

"As far as I can gather," said Sanders, "our friend is collecting a death-roll by the side of which the records of the Great Plague will read like an advertisement of a health resort."

"Where is he now?"

"He has got to Lukati—and I am worried"; and Sanders looked it.

The Houssa captain nodded, for all manner of reports had come down from Lukati country. There had been good crops, and good crops mean idleness, and idleness means mischief. Also there had been devil dances, and the mild people of the Bokari district, which lies contiguous to Lukati, had lost women.

"I've got a free hand to nip rebellion in the bud," Sanders reflected moodily; "and the chances point to rebellion——What do you say? Shall we make a report and wait for reinforcements, or shall we chance our luck?"

"It's your funeral," said the Houssa captain, "and I hate to advise you. If things go wrong you'll get the kicks; but if it were mine I'd go, like a shot—naturally."

"A hundred and forty men," mused Sanders.

"And two Maxims," suggested the other.

"We'll go," said Sanders; and half an hour later a bugle blared through the Houssas' lines, and Sanders was writing a report to his chief in far-away Lagos.

The Hon. George, it may be said, had no idea that he was anything but welcome in the village of Lukati.

Olari the chief had greeted him pleasantly, and told him stories of Sanders' brutality—stories which, as George wrote, "if true, must of necessity sound the death-knell of British integrity in our native possessions."

Exactly what that meant, I am not disposed to guess.

George stayed a month as the guest of Lukati. He had intended to stay at the most three days, but there was always a reason for postponing his departure.

Once the carriers deserted, once the roads were not safe, once Olari asked him to remain that he might see his young men dance. George did not know that his escort of four Houssas were feeling uneasy, because his interpreter—as big a fool as himself—could not interpret omens. George knew nothing of the significance of a dance in which no less than six witch-doctors took part, or the history of the tumble-down hut that stood in solitude at one end of the village. Had he taken the trouble to search that hut, he would have found a table, a chair, and a truckle bed, and on the table a report, soiled with dust and rain, which began:

"I have the honour to inform your Excellency that the natives maintain their industrious and peaceable attitude."

For in this hut in his lifetime lived Carter, Deputy Commissioner; and the natives, with their superstitious regard for the dead, had moved nothing.

It was approaching the end of the month, when the Hon. George thought he detected in his host a certain scarcely-veiled insolence of tone, and in the behaviour of the villagers something more threatening.

The dances were a nightly occurrence now, and the measured stamping of feet, the clash of spear against cane shield, and the never-ending growl of the song the dancers sang, kept him awake at nights. Messengers came to Olari daily from long distances, and once he was awakened in the middle of the night by screams. He jumped out of bed and pushed aside the fly of his tent to see half a dozen naked women dragged through the streets—the result of a raid upon the unoffending Bokari. He dressed, in a sweat of indignation and fear, and went to the chief's hut, fortunately without his interpreter, for what Olari said would have paralysed him.

In the morning (after this entirely unsatisfactory interview) he paraded his four Houssas and such of his carriers as he could find, and prepared to depart.

"Master," said Olari, when the request was interpreted, "I would rather you stayed. The land is full of bad people, and I have still much to tell you of the devilishness of Sandi. Moreover," said the chief, "to-night there is to be a great dance in your honour," and he pointed to where three slaves were engaged in erecting a big post in the centre of the village street.

"After this I will let you go," said Olari, "for you are my father and my mother."

The Hon. George was hesitating, when, of a sudden, at each end of the street there appeared, as if by magic, twenty travel-stained Houssas. They stood at attention for a moment, then opened outwards, and in the centre of each party gleamed the fat water-jacket of a Maxim gun.

The chief said nothing, only he looked first one way and then the other, and his brown face went a dirty grey. Sanders strolled leisurely along toward the group. He was unshaven, his clothes were torn with bush-thorn, in his hand was a long-barrelled revolver.

"Olari," he said gently; and the chief stepped forward.

"I think, Olari," said Sanders, "you have been chief too long."

"Master, my father was chief before me, and his father," said Olari, his face twitching.

"What of Tagondo, my friend?" asked Sanders, speaking of Carter by his native name.

"Master, he died," said Olari; "he died of the sickness *mongo*—the sickness itself."

"Surely," said Sanders, nodding his head, "surely you also shall die of the same sickness."

Olari looked round for a way of escape.

He saw the Hon. George looking from one to the other in perplexity, and he flung himself at the correspondent's feet.

"Master!" he cried, "save me from this man who hates me!"

George understood the gesture; his interpreter told him the rest; and, as a Houssa servant reached out his hand to the chief, the son of the house of Widnes, strong in the sense of his righteousness, struck it back.

"Look here, Sanders," forgetting all his previous misgivings and fears concerning the chief, "I should say that you have punished this poor devil enough!"

"Take that man, sergeant," said Sanders sharply; and the Houssa gripped Olari by the shoulder and flung him backward.

"You shall answer for this!" roared the Hon. George Tackle, in impotent wrath. "What are you going to do with him? My God! No, no!—not without a trial!"

He sprang forward, but the Houssas caught him and restrained him.

"For what you have done," said the correspondent—this was a month after, and he was going aboard the homeward steamer—"you shall suffer!"

"I only wish to point out to you," said Sanders, "that if I had not arrived in the nick of time, you would have done all the suffering—they were going to sacrifice you on the night I arrived. Didn't you see the post?"

"That is a lie!" said the other. "I will make England ring with your infamy. The condition of your district is a blot on civilisation!"

"There is no doubt," said Mr. Justice Keneally, summing up in the libel action, Sanders v. *The Courier and Echo* and another, "that the defendant Tackle did write a number of very libellous and damaging statements, and, to my mind, the most appalling aspect of the case is that, commissioned as he was to investigate the condition of affairs in the district of Lukati, he did not even trouble to find out where Lukati was. As you have been told, gentlemen of the jury, there are no less than four Lukatis in West Africa, the one in Togoland being the district in which it was intended the defendant should go. How he came to mistake Lukati of British West Africa for the Lukati of German Togoland, I do not know, but in order to bolster up his charges against a perfectly-innocent British official he brought forward a number of unsupported statements, each of which must be regarded as damaging to the plaintiff, but more damaging still to the newspaper that in its colossal ignorance published them."

The jury awarded Sanders nine thousand seven hundred and fifty pounds.

CHAPTER VI.
THE DANCING STONES.

Heroes should be tall and handsome, with flashing eyes; Sanders was not so tall, was yellow of face, moreover had grey hair. Heroes should also be of gentle address, full of soft phrases, for such tender women who come over their horizon; Sanders was a dispassionate man who swore on the slightest provocation, and had no use for women any way.

When you place a man upon a throne, even though that throne be a wooden stool worth in the mart fourpence more or less, you assume a responsibility which greatly outweighs all the satisfaction or personal gratification you may derive from your achievement. There is a grave in Toledo, a slab of brass, over a great king-maker who lived long enough to realise his insignificance. The epitaph upon that brass tomb of his is eloquent of his sum knowledge of life and human effort.

PULVIS
ET
NIHIL

says the inscription, and Powder and Nothing is the ultimate destiny of all king-makers.

Sanders was a maker of kings in the early days. He helped break a few, so it was in obedience to the laws of compensation that he took his part in reconstructive work.

He broke Esindini, Matabini, T'saki—to name three—and helped, in the very old days, and in another country, to break Lobengula, the Great Bull.

King-maker he was beyond question—you could see Republicanism written legibly in the amused grin with which he made them—but the kings he made were little ones—that is the custom of the British-African rule, they break a big king and put many little kings in his place, because it is much safer.

Somewhere about 12° north, and in longitude 0°, is a land which is peculiar for the fact that it is British, French, German, and Italian—according to which map of Africa you judge it by.

At the time of which I write it was neither, but it was ruled by Mensikilimbili for the Great King. He was the most powerful of monarchs, and, for the matter of that, the most cruel. His dominion stretched "from moonrise to sunset," said the natives, and he held undisputed sway.

He had a court, and sat upon an ivory throne, and wore over the leopard skins of his rank a mantle woven of gold thread and scarlet thread, and he administered justice. He had three hundred wives and forty thousand fighting men, and his acquaintance with white men began and ended with the coming of a French Mission, who presented him with a tall hat, a barrel organ, and one hundred thousand francs in gold.

This was Limbili, the great King of Yitingi.

The little kings of the Southern lands spoke of him with bated breath; his name was uttered in a low voice, as of a god; he was the symbol of majesty and of might—the Isisi people, themselves a nation of some importance, and boastful likewise, referred to themselves disparagingly when the kingdom of Yitingi was mentioned.

Following the French Mission, Sanders went up as envoy to the Limbilu, carrying presents of a kind and messages of good will.

He was escorted into the territory by a great army and was lodged in the city of the king. After two days' waiting he was informed that his Majesty would see him, and was led to the Presence.

The Presence was an old man, a vicious old man, if Sanders was any judge of character, who showed unmistakable signs of anger and contempt when the Commissioner displayed his presents.

"And what are these, white man?" said the king. "Toys for my women, or presents for my little chiefs?"

"These are for your Greatness," said Sanders quietly, "from a people who do not gauge friendship by the costliness of presents."

The king gave a little sniff.

"Tell me, white man," he said; "in your travels have you ever seen so great a king as I?"

"Lord king," said Sanders, frank to a fault. "I have seen greater."

The king frowned, and the crowd about his sacred person muttered menacingly.

"There you lie," said the king calmly; "for there never was a greater king than I."

"Let the white man say who is greater," croaked an aged councillor, and a murmur of approval arose.

"Lord," said Sanders, looking into the eyes of the old man who sat on the throne, "I have seen Lo Ben."[2]

The king frowned again, and nodded.

"Of him I have heard," he said; "he was a great king and an eater-up of nations—who else?"

"King," lied Sanders, "also Ketcewayo"; and something like a hush fell upon the court, for the name of Ketcewayo was one that travelled north.

"But of white kings," persisted the chief; "is there a white king in the world whose word when it goes forth causes men to tremble?"

Sanders grinned internally, knowing such a king, but answered that in all his life he had never met such a king.

"And of armies," said the king, "have you ever seen an army such as mine?"

And so through the category of his possessions he ran; and Sanders, finding that the lie was to save himself a great deal of trouble, lied and acclaimed King Limbili as the greatest king in all the world, commander of the most perfect army, ruler of a sublime kingdom.

It may be said that the kingdom of Yitingi owed its integrity to its faults, for, satisfied with the perfection of all his possessions, the great king confined his injustices, his cruelties, and his little wars within the boundaries of his state. Also he sought relaxation therein.

One day, just after the rains, when the world was cool and the air filled with the faint scent of African spring, Sanders made a tour through the little provinces. These are those lands which lie away from the big rivers. Countries curled up in odd corners, bisected sharply on the map by this or that international boundary line, or scattered on the fringe of the wild country vaguely inscribed by the chartographer as "Under British Influence."

It was always an interesting journey—Sanders made it once a year—for the way led up strange rivers and through unfamiliar scenes, past villages where other white men than Sanders were never seen. After a month's travel the Commissioner came to Icheli, which lies on the border of the great king's domain, and with immense civility he was received by the elders and the chiefs.

"Lord, you have come at a good moment," said the chief solemnly, "to-night Daihili dances."

"And who is Daihili?" asked Sanders.

They told him; later they brought for his inspection a self-conscious girl, a trifle pert, he thought, for a native.

A slim girl, taller than the average woman, with a figure perfectly modelled, a face not unpleasant even from the European standpoint, graceful in carriage, her every movement harmonious. Sanders, chewing the end of his cigar, took her in at one glance.

"My girl, they tell me that you dance," he said.

"That is so, master," she said; "I am the greatest dancer in all the world."

"So far I cannot go," said the cautious Commissioner; "but I do not doubt that your dancing is very wonderful."

"Lord," she said, with a gesture, "when I dance men go mad, losing their senses. To-night when the moon is high I will show you the dance of the Three Lovers."

"To-night," said Sanders briefly, "I shall be in bed—and, I trust, asleep."

The girl frowned a little, was possibly piqued, being a woman of fifteen, and in no wise different to women elsewhere in the world. This Sanders did not know, and I doubt whether the knowledge would have helped him much if he did.

He heard the tom-tom beating, that night as he lay in bed, and the rhythmical clapping of hands, and fell asleep wondering what would be the end of a girl who danced so that men went mad.

The child was the chief's daughter, and at parting Sanders had a few words to say concerning her.

"This daughter of yours is fifteen, and it would be better if she were married," he said.

"Lord, she has many lovers, but none rich enough to buy her," said the proud father, "because she is so great a dancer. Chiefs and headmen from villages far distant come to see her." He looked round and lowered his voice. "It is said," he whispered, "that the Great One himself has spoken of her. Perhaps he will send for her, offering this and that. In such a case," said the chief hopefully, "I will barter and bargain, keeping him in suspense, and every day the price will rise——"

"If the Great One need her, let her go," said Sanders, "lest instead of money presents he sends an army. I will have no war, or women palaver, which is worse than war, in my country—mark that, chief."

"Lord, your word is my desire," said the chief conventionally.

Sanders went back to his own people by easy stages. At Isisi he was detained for over a week over a question of witch-craft; at Belembi (in the Isisi country) he stopped three days to settle a case of murder by fetish. He was delivering judgment, and Abiboo, the Sergeant of Police, was selecting and testing his stoutest cane for the whipping which was to follow, when the chief of the Icheli came flying down the river with three canoes, and Sanders, who, from where he sat, commanded an uninterrupted view of the river, knew there was trouble—and guessed what that trouble was.

"Justice!" demanded the chief, his voice trembling with the rage and fear he had nursed, "justice against the Old One, the stealer of girls, the destroyer of cities—may death go to him. Iwa!——"

The very day Sanders had left, the messenger of the great king had come, and with him a hundred warriors, demanding the dancing girl. True to his pre-arranged scheme, the chief began the inevitable bargaining over terms. The presents offered were too small. The girl was worth a hundred thousand rods—nay, a thousand bags of salt.

"You were mad," said Sanders calmly; "no woman is worth a thousand bags of salt."

"Well, that might be," admitted the outraged father; "yet it would be folly to begin by naming a price too low. The bargaining went on through the night and all the next day, and in the end the envoy of the great king grew impatient.

"Let the woman be sent for," he said, and obedient to the summons came Daihili, demure enough, yet with covert glances of encouragement to the unemotional ambassador, and with subtle exhibitions of her charms.

"Woman," said the messenger, "the greatest of kings desires you, will you come?"

"Lord," said the girl, "I wish for nothing better."

With that, the hundred armed warriors in attendance at the palaver closed round the girl.

"And so," said Sanders, "you got nothing?"

"Lord, it is as you say," moaned the old chief.

"It is evident," said Sanders, "that an injustice has been done; for no man may take a woman unless he pay. I think," he added, with a flash of that mordant humour which occasionally illuminated his judgments, "that the man pays twice, once to the father, and all his life to his wife—but that is as may be."

Six weeks later, after consultation, Sanders sent a messenger to the great king, demanding the price of the woman.

What happened to the messenger I would rather not describe. That he was killed, is saying the least. Just before he died, when the glaze of death must have been on his eyes, and his poor wrecked body settling to the rest of oblivion, he was carried to a place before the king's hut, and Daihili danced the Dance of the Spirits. This much is now known.

Sanders did nothing; nor did the British Government, but hurried notes were exchanged between ambassadors and ministers in Paris, and that was the end of the incident.

Two Icheli spies went up into the great king's country. One came back saying that the dancing girl was the favourite wife of the old king, and that her whims swayed the destinies of the nation. Also he reported that because of this slim girl who danced, many men, councillors, and captains of war had died the death.

The other spy did not come back.

It may have been his discovery that induced the girl to send an army against the Icheli, thinking perchance that her people were spying upon her.

One day the city of Icheli was surrounded by the soldiers of the great king, and neither man, woman nor child escaped.

The news of the massacre did not come to Sanders for a long time. The reason was simple there was none to carry the message, for the Icheli are isolated folk. One day, however, an Isisi hunting party, searching for elephants, came upon a place where there was a smell of burning and many skeletons—and thus Sanders knew——

"We cannot," wrote Monsieur Leon Marchassa, Minister for Colonial Affairs, "accept responsibility for the misdoings of the king of the Yitingi, and my Government would regard with sympathetic interest any attempt that was made by His Majesty's Government to pacify this country."

But the British Government did nothing, because war is an expensive matter, and Sanders grinned and cursed his employers genially.

Taking his life in his hands, he went up to the border of Yitingi, with twenty policemen, and sent a messenger—a Yitingi messenger—to the king. With the audacity which was not the least of his assets, he demanded that the king should come to him for a palaver.

This adventure nearly proved abortive at the beginning, for just as the *Zaire* was steaming to the borders Sanders unexpectedly came upon traces of a raiding expedition. There were unmistakable signs as to the author.

"I have a mind to turn back and punish that cursed Bosambo, Chief of the Ochori," he said to Sergeant Abiboo, "for having sworn by a variety of gods and devils that he would keep the peace; behold he has been raiding in foreign territory."

"He will keep, master," said Abiboo, "besides which, he is in the neighbourhood, for his fires are still warm."

So Sanders went on, and sent his message to the king.

He kept steam in his little boat—he had chosen the only place where the river touches the Yitingi border—and waited, quite prepared to make an ignominious, if judicious, bolt.

To his astonishment, his spies brought word that the king was coming. He owed this condescension to the influence of the little dancing girl, for she, woman-like, had a memory for rebuffs, and had a score to settle with Mr. Commissioner Sanders.

The great king arrived, and across the meadow-like lands that fringe the river on both sides Sanders watched the winding procession with mingled feelings. The king halted a hundred yards from the river, and his big scarlet umbrella was the centre of a black line of soldiers spreading out on either hand for three hundred yards.

Then a party detached itself and came towards the dead tree by the water side, whereon hung limply in the still air the ensign of England.

"This," said Sanders to himself, "is where I go dead one time."

It is evidence of the seriousness of the situation, as it appealed to him, that he permitted himself to descend to Coast English.

"The king, the Great One, awaits you, white man, offering you safety in his shadow," said the king's messenger; and Sanders nodded. He walked leisurely toward the massed troops, and presently appeared before the old man squatting on a heap of skins and blinking like an ape in the sunlight.

"Lord king, live for ever," said Sanders glibly, and as he raised his hand in salute he saw the girl regarding him from under knit brows.

"What is your wish, white man?" said the old king; "what rich presents do you bring, that you call me many days' journey?"

"Lord, I bring no presents," said Sanders boldly; "but a message from a king who is greater than you, whose soldiers outnumber the sands of the river, and whose lands extend from the east to the west, from the north to the south."

"There is no such king," snarled the old man. "You lie, white man, and I will cut your tongue into little strips."

"Let him give his message, master," said the girl.

"This is the message," said Sanders. He stood easily, with his hands in the pockets of his white uniform jacket, and the king was nearer death than he knew. "My master says: 'Because the Great King of Yitingi has eaten up the Icheli folk: because he has crossed the borderland and brought suffering to my people, my heart is sore. Yet, if the Great King will pay a fine of one thousand head of cattle and will allow free access to his country for my soldiers and my commissioners, I will live in peace with him.'"

The old man laughed, a wicked, cackling laugh.

"Oh, ko!" he chuckled; "a great king!"

Then the girl stepped forward.

"Sandi," she said, "once you put me to shame, for when I would have danced for you, you slept."

"To you, Daihili," said Sanders steadily, "I say nothing; I make no palaver with women, for that is not the custom or the law. Still less do I talk with dancing girls. My business is with Limbili the king."

The king was talking rapidly behind his hand to a man who bent over him, and Sanders, his hands still in his jacket pockets, snapped down the safety catches of his automatic Colts.

All the time the girl spoke he was watching from the corners of his eyes the man who talked with the king. He saw him disappear in the crowd of soldiers who stood behind the squatting figures, and prepared for the worst.

"Since I may not dance for you," the girl was saying, "my lord the king would have you dance for me."

"That is folly," said Sanders: then he saw the line on either side wheel forward, and out came his pistols.

"Crack! Crack!"

The shot intended for the king missed him, and broke the leg of a soldier behind.

It had been hopeless from the first; this Sanders realised with some philosophy, as he lay stretched on the baked earth, trussed like a fowl, and exceedingly uncomfortable. At the first shot Abiboo, obeying his instructions, would turn the bows of the steamer down stream; this was the only poor satisfaction he could derive from the situation.

Throughout that long day, with a pitiless sun beating down upon him, he lay in the midst of an armed guard, waiting for the death which must come in some dreadful form or other.

He was undismayed, for this was the logical end of the business. Toward the evening they gave him water, which was most acceptable. From the gossip of his guards he gathered that the evening had been chosen for his exit, but the manner of it he must guess.

From where he lay he could see, by turning his head a little, the king's tent, and all the afternoon men were busily engaged in heaping flat stones upon the earth before the pavilion. They were of singular uniformity, and would appear to be specially hewn and dressed for some purpose. He asked his guard a question.

"They are the dancing stones, white man," said the soldier, "they come from the mountain near the city."

When darkness fell a huge fire was lit; it was whilst he was watching this that he heard of the *Zaire's* escape, and was thankful.

He must have been dozing, exhausted in body and mind, when he was dragged to his feet, his bonds were slipped, and he was led before the king. Then he saw what form his torture was to take.

The flat stones were being taken from the fire with wooden pincers and laid to form a rough pavement before the tent.

"White man," said the king, as rude hands pulled off the Commissioner's boots, "the woman Daihili would see you dance."

"Be assured, king," said Sanders, between his teeth, "that some day you shall dance in hell in more pleasant company, having first danced at the end of a rope."

"If you live through the dancing," said the king, "you will be sorry."

A ring of soldiers with their spears pointing inward surrounded the pavement, those on the side of the tent crouching so that their bodies might not interrupt the Great One's view.

"Dance," said the king; and Sanders was thrown forward. The first stone he touched was only just warm, and on this he stood still till a spear-thrust sent him to the next. It was smoking hot, and he leapt up with a stifled cry. Down he came to another, hotter still, and leapt again—

"Throw water over him," said the amused king, when they dragged the fainting man off the stones, his clothes smouldering where he lay in an inert heap.

"Now dance," said the king again—when out of the darkness about the group leapt a quivering pencil of yellow light.

Ha-ha-ha-ha-a-a-a!

Abiboo's Maxim-gun was in action at a range of fifty yards, and with him five hundred Ochori men under that chief of chiefs, Bosambo.

For a moment the Yitingi stood, and then, as with a wild yell which was three-parts fear, the Ochori charged, the king's soldiers broke and fled.

They carried Sanders to the steamer quickly, for the Yitingi would re-form, being famous night fighters. Sanders, sitting on the deck of the steamer nursing his burnt feet and swearing gently, heard the scramble of the Ochori as they got into their canoes, heard the grunting of his Houssas hoisting the Maxim on board, and fainted again.

"Master," said Bosambo in the morning, "many moons ago you made charge against the Ochori, saying they would not fight. That was true, but in those far-off days there was no chief Bosambo. Now, because of my teaching, and because I have put fire into their stomachs, they have defeated the soldiers of the Great King."

He posed magnificently, for on his shoulders was a mantle of gold thread woven with blue, which was not his the night before.

"Bosambo," said Sanders, "though I have a score to settle with you for breaking the law by raiding, I am grateful that the desire for the properties of others brought you to this neighbourhood. Where did you get that cloak?" he demanded.

"I stole it," said Bosambo frankly, "from the tent of the Great King; also I brought with me one of the stones upon which my lord would not stand. I brought this, thinking that it would be evidence."

Sanders nodded, and bit his cigar with a little grimace. "On which my lord would not stand," was very prettily put.

"Let me see it," he said; and Bosambo himself carried it to him.

It had borne the heat well enough, but rough handling had chipped a corner; and Sanders looked at this cracked corner long and earnestly.

"Here," he said, "is an argument that no properly constituted British Government can overlook—I see Limbili's finish."

The rainy season came round and the springtime, before Sanders again stood in the presence of the Great King. All around him was desolation and death. The plain was strewn with the bodies of men, and the big city was a smoking ruin. To the left, three regiments of Houssas were encamped; to the right, two battalions of African Rifles sat at "chop," and the snappy notes of their bugles came sharply through the still air.

"I am an old man," mumbled the king; but the girl who crouched at his side said nothing. Only her eyes never left the brick-red face of Sanders.

"Old you are," he said, "yet not too old to die."

"I am a great king," whined the other, "and it is not proper that a great king should hang."

"Yet if you live," said Sanders, "many other great kings will say, 'We may commit these abominations, and because of our greatness we shall live.'"

"And what of me, lord?" said the girl in a low voice.

"You!" Sanders looked at her. "Ho, hi," he said, as though he had just remembered her. "You are the dancing girl? Now we shall do nothing with you, Daihili—because you are nothing."

He saw her shrink as one under a lash.

After the execution, the Colonel of the Houssas and Sanders were talking together.

"What I can't understand," said the Colonel, "is why we suddenly decided upon this expedition. It has been necessary for years—but why this sudden activity?"

Sanders grinned mysteriously.

"A wonderful people, the English," he said airily. "Old Man Limbili steals British subjects, and I report it. 'Very sad,' says England. He wipes out a nation. 'Deplorable!' says England. He makes me dance on the original good-intention stones of Hades. 'Treat it as a joke,' says England; but when I point out that these stones assay one ounce ten penny-weights of refined gold, and that we've happed upon the richest reef in Central Africa, there's an army here in six months!"

I personally think that Sanders may have been a little unjust in his point of view. After all, wars cost money, and wars of vengeance are notoriously unprofitable.

CHAPTER VII.
THE FOREST OF HAPPY DREAMS.

Sanders was tied up at a "wooding," being on his way to collect taxes and administer justice to the folk who dwell on the lower Isisi River.

By the river-side the little steamer was moored. There was a tiny bay here, and the swift currents of the river were broken to a gentle flow; none the less, he inspected the shore-ends of the wire hawsers before he crossed the narrow plank that led to the deck of the *Zaire*. The wood was stacked on the deck, ready for to-morrow's run. The new water-gauge had been put in by Yoka, the engineer, as he had ordered; the engines had been cleaned; and Sanders nodded approvingly. He stepped lightly over two or three sleeping forms curled up on the deck, and gained the shore. "Now I think I'll turn in," he muttered, and looked at his watch. It was nine o'clock. He stood for a moment on the crest of the steep bank, and stared back across the river. The night was black, but he saw the outlines of the forest on the other side. He saw the jewelled sky, and the pale reflection of stars in the water. Then he went to his tent, and leisurely got into his pyjamas. He jerked two tabloids from a tiny bottle, swallowed them, drank a glass of water, and thrust his head through the tent opening. "Ho, Sokani!" he called, speaking in the vernacular, "let the *lo-koli* sound!"

He went to bed.

He heard the rustle of men moving, the gurgles of laughter as his subtle joke was repeated, for the Cambul people have a keen sense of humour, and then the penetrating rattle of sticks on the native drum—a hollow tree-trunk. Fiercely it beat—furiously, breathlessly, with now and then a deeper note as the drummer, using all his art, sent the message of sleep to the camp.

In one wild crescendo, the *lo-koli* ceased, and Sanders turned with a sigh of content and closed his eyes—he sat up suddenly. He must have dozed; but he was wide awake now.

He listened, then slipped out of bed, pulling on his mosquito boots. Into the darkness of the night he stepped, and found N'Kema, the engineer, waiting.

"You heard, master?" said the native.

"I heard," said Sanders, with a puzzled face, "yet we are nowhere near a village."

He listened.

From the night came a hundred whispering noises, but above all these, unmistakable, the faint clatter of an answering drum. The white man frowned in his perplexity. "No village is nearer than the Bongindanga," he muttered, "not even a fishing village; the woods are deserted——"

The native held up a warning finger, and bent his head, listening. He was reading the message that the drum sent. Sanders waited; he knew the wonderful fact of this native telegraph, how it sent news through the trackless wilds. He could not understand it, no European could; but he had respect for its mystery.

"A white man is here," read the native; "he has the sickness."

"A white man!"

In the darkness Sanders' eyebrows rose incredulously.

"He is a foolish one," N'Kema read; "he sits in the Forest of Happy Thoughts, and will not move."

Sanders clicked his lips impatiently. "No white man would sit in the Forest of Happy Thoughts," he said, half to himself, "unless he were mad."

But the distant drum monotonously repeated the outrageous news. Here, indeed, in the heart of the loveliest glade in all Africa, encamped in the very centre of the Green Path of Death, was a white man, a sick white man—in the Forest of Happy Thoughts—a sick white man.

So the drum went on and on, till Sanders, rousing his own *lo-koli* man, sent an answer crashing along the river, and began to dress hurriedly.

In the forest lay a very sick man. He had chosen the site for the camp himself. It was in a clearing, near a little creek that wound between high elephant-grass to the river. Mainward chose it, just before the sickness came, because it was pretty. This was altogether an inadequate reason; but Mainward was a sentimentalist, and his life was a long record of choosing pretty camping places, irrespective of danger. "He was," said a newspaper, commenting on the crowning disaster which sent him a fugitive from justice to the wild lands of Africa, "over-burdened with imagination." Mainward was cursed with ill-timed confidence; this was one of the reasons he chose to linger in that deadly strip of land of the Ituri, which is clumsily named by the natives "The Lands-where-all-bad-thoughts-become-good-thoughts" and poetically adapted by explorers and daring traders as "The Forest of Happy Dreams." Over-confidence had generally been Mainward's undoing—over-confidence in the ability of his horses to win races; over-confidence in his own ability to secure money to hide his defalcations—he was a director in the Welshire County Bank once—over-confidence in securing the love of a woman, who, when the crash came, looked at him blankly and said she was sorry, but she had no idea he felt towards her like that——

71

Now Mainward lifted his aching head from the pillow and cursed aloud at the din. He was endowed with the smattering of pigeon-English which a man may acquire from a three months' sojourn divided between Sierra Leone and Grand Bassam.

"Why for they make 'em cursed noise, eh?" he fretted. "You plenty fool-man, Abiboo."

"Si, senor," agreed the Kano boy, calmly.

"Stop it, d'ye hear? stop it!" raved the man on the tumbled bed; "this noise is driving me mad—tell them to stop the drum."

The *lo-koli* stopped of its own accord, for the listeners in the sick man's camp had heard the faint answer from Sanders.

"Come here, Abiboo—I want some milk; open a fresh tin; and tell the cook I want some soup, too."

The servant left him muttering and tossing from side to side on the creaking camp bedstead. Mainward had many strange things to think about. It was strange how they all clamoured for immediate attention; strange how they elbowed and fought one another in their noisy claims to his notice. Of course, there was the bankruptcy and the discovery at the bank—it was very decent of that inspector fellow to clear out—and Ethel, and the horses, and—and——

The Valley of Happy Dreams! That would make a good story if Mainward could write; only, unfortunately, he could not write. He could sign things, sign his name "three months after date pay to the order of——" He could sign other people's names; he groaned, and winced at the thought.

But here was a forest where bad thoughts became good, and, God knows, his mind was ill-furnished. He wanted peace and sleep and happiness—he greatly desired happiness. Now suppose "Fairy Lane" had won the Wokingham Stakes? It had not, of course (he winced again at the bad memory), but suppose it had? Suppose he could have found a friend who would have lent him £16,000, or even if Ethel——

"Master," said Abiboo's voice, "dem puck-a-puck, him lib for come."

"Eh, what's that?"

Mainward turned almost savagely on the man.

"Puck-a-puck—you hear'um?"

But the sick man could not hear the smack of the *Zaire*'s stern wheel, as the little boat breasted the downward rush of the river—he was surprised to see that it was dawn, and grudgingly admitted to himself that he had slept. He closed his eyes again and had a strange dream. The principal figure was a small, tanned, clean-shaven man in a white helmet, who wore a dingy yellow overcoat over his pyjamas.

"How are you feeling?" said the stranger.

"Rotten bad," growled Mainward, "especially about Ethel; don't you think it was pretty low down of her to lead me on to believe she was awfully fond of me, and then at the last minute to chuck me?"

"Shocking," said the strange, white man gravely, "but put her out of your mind just now; she isn't worth troubling about. What do you say to this?"

He held up a small, greenish pellet between his forefinger and thumb, and Mainward laughed weakly.

"Oh, rot!" he chuckled faintly. "You're one of those Forest of Happy Dreams Johnnies; what's that? A love philtre?" He was hysterically amused at the witticism.

Sanders nodded.

"Love or life, it's all one," he said, but apparently unamused. "Swallow it!"

Mainward giggled and obeyed.

"And now," said the stranger—this was six hours later—"the best thing you can do is to let my boys put you on my steamer and take you down river."

Mainward shook his head. He had awakened irritable and lamentably weak.

"My dear chap, it's awfully kind of you to have come—by the way, I suppose you *are* a doctor?"

Sanders shook his head.

"On the contrary, I am the Commissioner of this district," he said flippantly—"but you were saying——"

"I want to stay here—it's devilish pretty."

"Devilish is the very adjective I should have used—my dear man, this is the plague spot of the Congo; it's the home of every death-dealing fly and bug in Africa."

He waved his hand to the hidden vistas of fresh green glades, of gorgeous creepers shown in the light of the camp fires.

"Look at the grass," he said; "it's homeland grass—that's the seductive part of it; I nearly camped here myself. Come, my friend, let me take you to my camp."

Mainward shook his head obstinately.

"I'm obliged, but I'll stay here for a day or so. I want to try the supernatural effects of this pleasant place," he said with a weary smile. "I've got so many thoughts that need treatment."

"Look here," said Sanders roughly, "you know jolly well how this forest got its name; it is called Happy Dreams because it's impregnated with fever, and with every disease from beri-beri to sleeping sickness. You don't wake from the dreams you dream here. Man, I know this country, and you're a newcomer; you've trekked here because you wanted to get away from life and start all over again."

"I beg your pardon." Mainward's face flushed; and he spoke a little stiffly.

"Oh, I know all about you—didn't I tell you I was the Commissioner? I was in England when things were going rocky with you, and I've read the rest in the papers I get from time to time. But all that is nothing to me. I'm here to help you start fair. If you had wanted to commit suicide, why come to Africa to do it? Be sensible and shift your camp; I'll send my steamer back for your men. Will you come?"

"No," said Mainward sulkily. "I don't want to, I'm not keen; besides, I'm not fit to travel."

Here was an argument which Sanders could not answer. He was none too sure upon that point himself, and he hesitated before he spoke again.

"Very well," he said at length, "suppose you stay another day to give you a chance to pull yourself together. I'll come along to-morrow with a tip-top invalid chair for you—is it a bet?"

Mainward held out his shaking hand, and the ghost of a smile puckered the corners of his eyes. "It's a bet," he said.

He watched the Commissioner walk through the camp, speaking to one man after another in a strange tongue. A singular, masterful man this, thought Mainward. Would he have mastered Ethel? He watched the stranger with curious eyes, and noted how his own lazy devils of carriers jumped at his word.

"Good-night," said Sanders' voice; and Mainward looked up. "You must take another of these pellets, and to-morrow you'll be as fit as a donkey-engine. I've got to get back to my camp to-night, or I shall find half my stores stolen in the morning; but if you'd rather I stopped——"

"No, no," replied the other hastily. He wanted to be alone. He had lots of matters to settle with himself. There was the question of Ethel, for instance.

"You won't forget to take the tabloid?"

"No. I say, I'm awfully obliged to you for coming. You've been a good white citizen."

Sanders smiled. "Don't talk nonsense!" he said good-humouredly. "This is all brotherly love. White to white, and kin to kin, don't you know? We're all alone here, and there isn't a man of our colour within five hundred miles. Good-night, and please take the tabloid——"

Mainward lay listening to the noise of departure. He thought he heard a little bell tingle. That must be for the engines. Then he heard the puck-a-puck of the wheel—so that was how the steamer got its name.

Abiboo came with some milk. "You take um medicine, master?" he inquired.

"I take um," murmured Mainward; but the green tabloid was underneath his pillow.

Then there began to steal over him a curious sensation of content. He did not analyse it down to its first cause. He had had sufficient introspective exercise for one day. It came to him as a pleasant shock to realise that he was happy.

He opened his eyes and looked round.

His bed was laid in the open, and he drew aside the curtains of his net to get a better view.

A little man was walking briskly toward him along the velvet stretch of grass that sloped down from the glade, and Mainward whistled.

"Atty," he gasped. "By all that's wonderful."

Atty, indeed, it was: the same wizened Atty as of yore; but no longer pulling the long face to which Mainward had been accustomed. The little man was in his white riding-breeches, his diminutive top-boots were splashed with mud, and on the crimson of his silk jacket there was evidence of a hard race. He touched his cap jerkily with his whip, and shifted the burden of the racing saddle he carried to the other arm.

"Why, Atty," said Mainward, with a smile, "what on earth are you doing here?"

"It's a short way to the jockey's room, sir," said the little man. "I've just weighed in. I thought the Fairy would do it, sir, and she did."

Mainward nodded wisely. "I knew she would, too," he said.

"Did she give you a smooth ride?"

The jockey grinned again. "She never does that," he said. "But she ran gamely enough. Coming up out of the Dip, she hung a little, but I showed her the whip, and she came on as straight as a die. I thought once the Stalk would beat us—I got shut in, but I pulled her round, and we were never in difficulties. I could have won by ten lengths," said Atty.

"You could have won by ten lengths," repeated Mainward in wonder. "Well, you've done me a good turn, Atty. This win will get me out of one of the biggest holes that ever a reckless man tumbled into—I shall not forget you, Atty."

"I'm sure you won't, sir," said the little jockey gratefully; "if you'll excuse me now, sir——"

Mainward nodded and watched him, as he moved quickly through the trees.

There were several people in the glade now, and Mainward looked down ruefully at his soiled duck suit. "What an ass I was to come like this," he muttered in his annoyance. "I might have known that I should have met all these people."

There was one he did not wish to see; and as soon as he sighted Venn, with his shy eyes and his big nose, Mainward endeavoured to slip back out of observation. But Venn saw him, and came tumbling through the trees, with his big, flabby hand extended and his dull eyes aglow.

"Hullo, hullo!" he grinned, "been looking for you."

Mainward muttered some inconsequent reply. "Rum place to find you, eh?" Venn removed his shining silk hat and mopped his brow with an awesome silk handkerchief.

"But look here, old feller—about that money?"

"Don't worry, my dear man," Mainward interposed easily. "I shall pay you now."

"That ain't what I mean," said the other impetuously; "a few hundred more or less does not count. But you wanted a big sum——"

"And you told me you'd see me——"

"I know, I know," Venn put in hastily; "but that was before Kaffirs started jumpin'. Old feller, you can have it!"

He said this with grotesque emphasis, standing with his legs wide apart, his hat perched on the back of his head, his plump hands dramatically outstretched: and Mainward laughed outright.

"Sixteen thousand?" he asked.

"Or twenty," said the other impressively. "I want to show you——" Somebody called him, and with a hurried apology he went blundering up the green slope, stopping and turning back to indulge in a little dumb show illustrative of his confidence in Mainward and his willingness to oblige.

Mainward was laughing, a low, gurgling laugh of pure enjoyment. Venn, of all people! Venn, with his accursed questions and talk of securities. Well! Well!

Then his merriment ceases, and he winced again, and his heart beat faster and faster, and a curious weakness came over him——

How splendidly cool she looked.

She walked in the clearing, a white, slim figure; he heard the swish of her skirt as she came through the long grass—white, with a green belt all encrusted with gold embroidery. He took in every detail hungrily—the dangling gold ornaments that hung from her belt, the lace collar at her throat, the——

She did not hurry to him, that was not her way.

But in her eyes dawned a gradual tenderness—those dear eyes that dropped before his shyly.

"Ethel!" he whispered, and dared to take her hand.

"Aren't you wonderfully surprised?" she said.

"Ethel! Here!"

"I—I had to come."

She would not look at him, but he saw the pink in her cheek and heard the faltering voice with a wild hope. "I behaved so badly, dear—so very badly."

She hung her head.

"Dear! dear!" he muttered, and groped toward her like a blind man.

She was in his arms, crushed against his breast, the perfume of her presence in his brain.

"I had to come to you." Her hot cheek was against his. "I love you so."

"Me—love me? Do you mean it?" He was tremulous with happiness, and his voice broke—"Dearest."

Her face was upturned to his, her lips so near; he felt her heart beating as furiously as his own. He kissed her—her lips, her eyes, her dear hair——

"O, God, I'm happy!" she sobbed, "so—so happy——"

Sanders sprang ashore just as the sun was rising, and came thoughtfully through the undergrowth to the camp. Abiboo, squatting by the curtained bed, did not rise. Sanders walked to the bed, pulled aside the mosquito netting, and bent over the man who lay there.

Then he drew the curtains again, lit his pipe slowly, and looked down at Abiboo.

"When did he die?" he asked.

"In the dark of the morning, master," said the man.

Sanders nodded slowly. "Why did you not send for me?"

For a moment the squatting figure made no reply, then he rose and stretched himself.

"Master," he said, speaking in Arabic—which is a language which allows of nice distinctions—"this man was happy; he walked in the Forest of Happy Thoughts; why should I call him back to a land where there was neither sunshine nor happiness, but only night and pain and sickness?"

"You're a philosopher," said Sanders irritably.

"I am a follower of the Prophet," said Abiboo, the Kano boy; "and all things are according to God's wisdom."

CHAPTER VIII.
THE AKASAVAS.

You who do not understand how out of good evil may arise must take your spade to some virgin grassland, untouched by the hand of man from the beginning of time. Here is soft, sweet grass, and never a sign of nettle, or rank, evil weed. It is as God made it. Turn the soil with your spade, intent on improving His handiwork, and next season—weeds, nettles, lank creeping things, and coarse-leafed vegetation cover the ground.

Your spade has aroused to life the dormant seeds of evil, germinated the ugly waste life that all these long years has been sleeping out of sight—in twenty years, with careful cultivation, you may fight down the weeds and restore the grassland, but it takes a lot of doing.

Your intentions may have been the best in disturbing the primal sod; you may have had views of roses flourishing where grass was; the result is very much the same.

I apply this parable to the story of a missionary and his work. The missionary was a good man, though of the wrong colour. He had large ideas on his duty to his fellows; he was inspired by the work of his cloth in another country; but, as Sanders properly said, India is not Africa.

Kenneth McDolan came to Mr. Commissioner Sanders with a letter of introduction from the new Administration.

Sanders was at "chop" one blazing morning when his servant, who was also his sergeant, Abiboo, brought a card to him. It was a nice card, rounded at the corners, and gilt-edged, and in the centre, in old English type, was the inscription—

Rev. KENNETH McDOLAN.

Underneath was scribbled in pencil: "On a brief visit." Sanders sniffed impatiently, for "reverend" meant "missionary," and "missionary" might mean anything. He looked at the card again and frowned in his perplexity. Somehow the old English and the reverendness of the visiting card did not go well with the rounded corners and the gilt edge.

"Where is he?" he demanded.

"Master," said Abiboo, "he is on the verandah. Shall I kick him off?" Abiboo said this very naturally and with simple directness, and Sanders stared at him.

"Son of sin!" he said sternly, "is it thus you speak of God-men, and of white men at that?"

"This man wears the clothes of a God-man," said Abiboo serenely; "but he is a black man, therefore of no consequence."

Sanders pulled a pair of mosquito boots over his pyjamas and swore to himself.

"White missionaries, yes," he said wrathfully, "but black missionaries I will not endure."

The Reverend Kenneth was sitting in Sanders' basket-chair, one leg flung negligently over one side of the chair to display a silk sock. His finger-tips were

79

touching, and he was gazing with good-natured tolerance at the little green garden which was the Commissioner's special delight.

He was black, very black; but his manners were easy, and his bearing self-possessed.

He nodded smilingly to Sanders and extended a lazy hand.

"Ah, Mr. Commissioner," he said in faultless English, "I have heard a great deal about you."

"Get out of that chair," said Sanders, who had no small talk worth mentioning, "and stand up when I come out to you! What do you want?"

The Reverend Kenneth rose quickly, and accepted the situation with a rapidity which will be incomprehensible to any who do not know how thumbnail deep is the cultivation of the cultured savage.

"I am on a brief visit," he said, a note of deference in his tone. "I am taking the small towns and villages along the coast, holding services, and I desire permission to speak to your people."

This was not the speech he had prepared. He had come straight from England, where he had been something of a lion in Bayswater society, and where, too, his theological attainments had won him regard and no small amount of fame in even a wider circle.

"You may speak to my people," said Sanders; "but you may not address the Kano folk nor the Houssas, because they are petrified in the faith of the Prophet."

Regaining his self-possession, the missionary smiled.

"To bring light into dark places——" he began.

"Cut it out," said Sanders briefly; "the palaver is finished." He turned on his heel and re-entered the bungalow.

Then a thought struck him.

"Hi!" he shouted, and the retiring missionary turned back.

"Where did you pick up the 'Kenneth McDolan'?" he asked.

The negro smiled again.

"It is the patronymic bestowed upon me at Sierra Leone by a good Christian white man, who brought me up and educated me as though I were his own son," he recited.

Sanders showed his teeth.

"I have heard of such cases," he said unpleasantly.

The next day the missionary announced his intention of proceeding up country. He came in to see Sanders as though nothing had happened. Perhaps he expected to find the Commissioner a little ashamed of himself; but if this was so he was disappointed, for Sanders was blatantly unrepentant.

"You've got a letter from the Administration," he said, "so I can't stop you."

"There is work for me," said the missionary, "work of succour and relief. In India some four hundred thousand——"

"This is not India," said Sanders shortly; and with no other word the native preacher went his way.

Those who know the Akasava people best know them for their laziness—save in matter of vendetta, or in the settlement of such blood feuds as come their way, or in the lifting of each other's goats, in all which matters they display an energy and an agility truly inexplicable. "He is an Akasava man—he points with his foot," is a proverb of the Upper River, and the origin of the saying goes back to a misty time when (as the legend goes) a stranger happened upon a man of the tribe lying in the forest.

"Friend," said the stranger, "I am lost. Show me the way to the river"; and the Akasava warrior, raising a leg from the ground, pointed with his toe to the path.

Though this legend lacks something in point of humour, it is regarded as the acme of mirth-provoking stories from Bama to the Lado country.

It was six months after the Reverend Kenneth McDolan had left for his station that there came to Sanders at his headquarters a woeful deputation, arriving in two canoes in the middle of the night, and awaiting him when he came from his bath to the broad stoep of his house in the morning—a semi-circle of chastened and gloomy men, who squatted on the wooden stoep, regarding him with the utmost misery.

"Lord, we are of the Akasava people," said the spokesman, "and we have come a long journey."

"So I am aware," said Sanders, with acrid dryness, "unless the Akasava country has shifted its position in the night. What do you seek?"

"Master, we are starving," said the speaker, "for our crops have failed, and there is no fish in the river; therefore we have come to you, who are our father."

Now this was a most unusual request; for the Central African native does not easily starve, and, moreover, there had come no news of crop failure from the Upper River.

"All this sounds like a lie," said Sanders thoughtfully, "for how may a crop fail in the Akasava country, yet be more than sufficient in Isisi? Moreover, fish do not leave their playground without cause, and if they do they may be followed."

The spokesman shifted uneasily.

"Master, we have had much sickness," he said, "and whilst we cared for one another the planting season had passed; and, as for the fish, our young men were too full of sorrow for their dead to go long journeys." Sanders stared.

"Therefore we have come from our chief asking you to save us, for we are starving."

The man spoke with some confidence, and this was the most surprising thing of all. Sanders was nonplussed, frankly confounded. For all the eccentric course his daily life took, there was a certain regularity even in its irregularity. But here was a new and unfamiliar situation. Such things mean trouble, and he was about to probe this matter to its depth.

"I have nothing to give you," he said, "save this advice—that you return swiftly to where you came from and carry my word to your chief. Later I will come and make inquiries."

The men were not satisfied, and an elder, wrinkled with age, and sooty-grey of head, spoke up.

"It is said, master," he mumbled, through his toothless jaws, "that in other lands when men starve there come many white men bringing grain and comfort."

"Eh?"

Sanders' eyes narrowed.

"Wait," he said, and walked quickly through the open door of his bungalow.

When he came out he carried a pliant whip of rhinoceros-hide, and the deputation, losing its serenity, fled precipitately.

Sanders watched the two canoes paddling frantically up stream, and the smile was without any considerable sign of amusement. That same night the *Zaire* left for the Akasava country, carrying a letter to the Reverend Kenneth McDolan, which was brief, but unmistakable in its tenor.

"DEAR SIR,"—it ran—"You will accompany the bearer to headquarters, together with your belongings. In the event of your refusing to comply with this request, I have instructed my sergeant to arrest you. Yours faithfully,

"And the reason I am sending you out of this country," said Sanders, "is because you have put funny ideas into the heads of my people."

"I assure you——" began the negro.

"I don't want your assurance," said Sanders, "you are not going to work an Indian Famine Fund in Central Africa."

"The people were starving——"

Sanders smiled.

"I have sent word to them that I am coming to Akasava," he said grimly, "and that I will take the first starved-looking man I see and beat him till he is sore."

The next day the missionary went, to the intense relief, be it said, of the many white missionaries scattered up and down the river; for, strange as it may appear, a negro preacher who wears a black coat and silk socks is regarded with a certain amount of suspicion.

True to his promise, Sanders made his visit, but found none to thrash, for he came to a singularly well-fed community that had spent a whole week in digging out of the secret hiding-places the foodstuffs which, at the suggestion of a too zealous seeker after fame, it had concealed.

"Here," said Sanders, wickedly, "endeth the first lesson."

But he was far from happy. It is a remarkable fact that once you interfere with the smooth current of native life all manner of things happen. It cannot be truthfully said that the events that followed on the retirement from active life of the Reverend Kenneth McDolan were immediately traceable to his ingenious attempt to engineer a famine in Akasava. But he had sown a seed, the seed of an idea that somebody was responsible for their well-being—he had set up a beautiful idol of Pauperism, a new and wonderful fetish. In the short time of his stay he had instilled into the heathen mind the dim, vague, and elusive idea of the Brotherhood of Man.

This Sanders discovered, when, returning from his visit of inspection, he met, drifting with the stream, a canoe in which lay a prone man, lazily setting his course with half-hearted paddle strokes.

Sanders, on the bridge of his tiny steamer, pulled the little string that controlled the steam whistle, for the canoe lay in his track. Despite the warning, the man in the canoe made no effort to get out of his way, and since both were going with the current, it was only by putting the wheel over and scraping a sandbank that the steamer missed sinking the smaller craft.

"Bring that man on board!" fumed Sanders, and when the canoe had been unceremoniously hauled to the *Zaire's* side by a boat-hook, and the occupant rudely pulled on board, Sanders let himself go.

"By your infernal laziness," he said, "I see that you are of the Akasava people; yet that is no reason why you should take the middle of the channel to yourself."

"Lord, it is written in the books of your gods," said the man, "that the river is for us all, black and white, each being equal in the eyes of the white gods."

Sanders checked his lips impatiently.

"When you and I are dead," he said, "we shall be equal, but since I am quick and you are quick, I shall give you ten strokes with a whip to correct the evil teaching that is within you."

He made a convert.

But the mischief was done.

Sanders knew the native mind much better than any man living, and he spent a certain period every day for the next month cursing the Reverend Kenneth McDolan. So far, however, no irreparable mischief had been done, but Sanders was not the kind of man to be caught napping. Into the farthermost corners of his little kingdom his secret-service men were dispatched, and Sanders sat down to await developments.

At first the news was good; the spies sent back stories of peace, of normal happiness; then the reports became less satisfactory. The Akasava country is unfortunately placed, for it is the very centre territory, the ideal position for the dissemination of foolish propaganda, as Sanders had discovered before.

The stories the spies sent or brought were of secret meetings, of envoys from tribe to tribe, envoys that stole out from villages by dead of night, of curious rites performed in the depth of the forest and other disturbing matters.

Then came a climax.

Tigili, the king of the N'Gombi folk, made preparations for a secret journey. He sacrificed a goat and secured good omens; likewise three witch-doctors in solemn conclave gave a favourable prophecy.

The chief slipped down the river one night with fourteen paddlers, a drummer, his chief headsman, and two of his wives, and reached the Akasava city at sunset the next evening. Here the chief of the Akasava met him, and led him to his hut.

"Brother," said the Akasava chief, not without a touch of pompousness, "I have covered my bow with the skin of a monkey."

Tigili nodded gravely.

"My arrows are winged with the little clouds," he said in reply.

In this cryptic fashion they spoke for the greater part of an hour, and derived much profit therefrom.

In the shadow of the hut without lay a half-naked man, who seemed to sleep, his head upon his arm, his legs doubled up comfortably.

One of the Akasava guard saw him, and sought to arouse him with the butt of his spear, but he only stirred sleepily, and, thinking that he must be a man of Tigili's retinue, they left him.

When the king and the chief had finished their palaver, Tigili rose from the floor of the hut and went back to his canoe, and the chief of the Akasava stood on the bank of the river watching the craft as it went back the way it had come.

The sleeper rose noiselessly and took another path to the river. Just outside the town he had to cross a path of moonlit clearing, and a man challenged him.

This man was an Akasava warrior, and was armed, and the sleeper stood obedient to the summons.

"Who are you?"

"I am a stranger," said the man.

The warrior came nearer and looked in his face.

"You are a spy of Sandi," he said, and then the other closed with him.

The warrior would have shouted, but a hand like steel was on his throat. The sentinel made a little sound like the noise a small river makes when it crosses a shallow bed of shingle, then his legs bent limply, and he went down.

The sleeper bent down over him, wiped his knife on the bare shoulder of the dead man, and went on his way to the river. Under the bush he found a canoe, untied the native rope that fastened it, and stepping in, he sent the tiny dug-out down the stream.

"And what do you make of all this?" asked Sanders. He was standing on his broad stoep, and before him was the spy, a lithe young man, in the uniform of a sergeant of Houssa Police.

"Master, it is the secret society, and they go to make a great killing," said the sergeant.

The Commissioner paced the verandah with his head upon his breast, his hands clasped behind his back.

These secret societies he knew well enough, though his territories had been free of them. He knew their mushroom growth; how they rose from nothingness with rituals and practices ready-made. He knew their influence up and down the Liberian coast; he had some knowledge of the "silent ones" of Nigeria, and had met the "white faces" in the Kassai. And now the curse had come to his territory. It meant war, the upsetting of twenty years' work—the work of men who died and died joyfully, in the faith that they had brought peace to the land—it meant the undermining of all his authority.

He turned to Abiboo.

"Take the steamer," he said, "and go quickly to the Ochori country, telling Bosambo, the chief, that I will come to him—the palaver is finished." He knew he could depend upon Bosambo if the worst came.

In the days of waiting he sent a long message to the Administration, which lived in ease a hundred miles down the coast. He had a land wire running along the seashore, and when it worked it was a great blessing. Fortunately it was in good order now, but there had been times when wandering droves of elephants had pulled up the poles and twisted a mile or so of wire into a hopeless tangle.

The reply to his message came quickly.

"Take extreme steps to wipe out society. If necessary arrest Tigili. I will support you with four hundred men and a gunboat; prefer you should arrange the matter without fuss.

Sanders took a long walk by the sea to think out the situation and the solution. If the people were preparing for war, there would be simultaneous action, a general rising. He shook his head. Four hundred men and a gunboat more or less would make no difference. There was a hope that one tribe would rise before the other; he could deal with the Akasava; he could deal with the Isisi plus the Akasava; he was sure of the Ochori—that was a comfort—but the others? He shook his head again. Perhaps the inherent idleness of the Akasava would keep them back. Such a possibility was against their traditions.

He must have come upon a solution suddenly, for he stopped dead in his walk, and stood still, thinking profoundly, with his head upon his breast. Then he turned and walked quickly back to his bungalow.

What date had been chosen for the rising we may never know for certain. What is known is that the Akasava, the N'Gombi, the Isisi, and the Boleki folk were preparing in secret for a time of killing, when there came the great news.

Sandi was dead.

A canoe had overturned on the Isisi River, and the swift current had swept the Commissioner away, and though men ran up and down the bank no other sign of him was visible but a great white helmet that floated, turning slowly, out of sight.

So a man of the Akasava reported, having learnt it from a sergeant of Houssas, and instantly the *lo-koli* beat sharply, and the headmen of the villages came panting to the palaver house to meet the paramount chief of the Akasava.

"Sandi is dead," said the chief solemnly. "He was our father and our mother and carried us in his arms; we loved him and did many disagreeable things for him because of our love. But now that he is dead, and there is none to say 'Yea' or 'Nay' to us, the time of which I have spoken to you secretly has come; therefore let us take up our arms and go out, first against the God-men who pray and bewitch us with the sprinkling of water, then against the chief of the Ochori, who for many years have put shame upon us."

"Master," said a little chief from the fishing village which is near to the Ochori border, "is it wise—our Lord Sandi having said there shall be no war?"

"Our Lord Sandi is dead," said the paramount chief wisely; "and being dead, it does not greatly concern us what he said; besides which," he said, as a thought struck him, "last night I had a dream and saw Sandi; he was standing amidst great fires, and he said, 'Go forth and bring me the head of the chief of the Ochori.'"

No further time was wasted.

That night the men of twenty villages danced the dance of killing, and the great fire of the Akasava burnt redly on the sandy beach to the embarrassment of a hippo family that lived in the high grasses near by.

In the grey of the morning the Akasava chief mustered six hundred spears and three score of canoes, and he delivered his oration:

"First, we will destroy the mission men, for they are white, and it is not right that they should live and Sandi be dead; then we will go against Bosambo, the chief of the Ochori. When rains came in the time of kidding, he who is a foreigner and of no human origin brought many evil persons with him and destroyed our fishing villages, and Sandi said there should be no killing. Now Sandi is dead, and, I do not doubt, in hell, and there is none to hold our pride."

Round the bend of the river, ever so slowly, for she was breasting a strong and treacherous current, came the nose of the *Zaire*. It is worthy of note that the little blue flag at her stern was not at half-mast. The exact significance of this was lost on the Akasava. Gingerly the little craft felt its way to the sandy strip of beach, a plank was thrust forth, and along it came, very dapper and white, his little ebony stick with the silver knob swinging between his fingers, Mr. Commissioner Sanders, very much alive, and there were two bright Maxim-guns on either side of the gangway that covered the beach.

A nation, paralysed by fear and apprehension, watched the *debarquement*, the chief of the Akasava being a little in advance of his painted warriors.

On Sanders' face was a look of innocent surprise. "Chief," said he, "you do me great honour that you gather your young men to welcome me; nevertheless, I would rather see them working in their gardens."

He walked along one row of fighting men, plentifully besmeared with cam-wood, and his was the leisurely step of some great personage inspecting a guard of honour.

"I perceive," he went on, talking over his shoulder to the chief who, fascinated by the unexpected vision, followed him, "I perceive that each man has a killing spear, also a fighting shield of wicker work, and many have N'Gombi swords."

"Lord, it is true," said the chief, recovering his wits, "for we go hunting elephant in the Great Forest."

"Also that some have the little bones of men fastened about their necks—that is not for the elephant."

He said this meditatively, musingly, as he continued his inspection, and the chief was frankly embarrassed.

"There is a rumour," he stammered, "it is said—there came a spy who told us—that the Ochori were gathering for war, and we were afraid——"

"Strange," said Sanders, half to himself, but speaking in the vernacular, "strange indeed is this story, for I have come straight from the Ochori city, and there I saw nothing but men who ground corn and hunted peacefully; also their chief is ill, suffering from a fever."

He shook his head in well-simulated bewilderment.

"Lord," said the poor chief of the Akasava, "perhaps men have told us lies—such things have happened——"

"That is true," said Sanders gravely. "This is a country of lies; some say that I am dead; and, lo! the news has gone around that there is no law in the land, and men may kill and war at their good pleasure."

"Though I die at this minute," said the chief virtuously, "though the river turn to fire and consume my inmost stomach, though every tree become a tiger to devour me, I have not dreamt of war."

Sanders grinned internally.

"Spare your breath," he said gently. "You who go hunting elephants, for it is a long journey to the Great Forest, and there are many swamps to be crossed, many rivers to be swum. My heart is glad that I have come in time to bid you farewell."

There was a most impressive silence, for this killing of elephants was a stray excuse of the chief's. The Great Forest is a journey of two months, one to get there and one to return, and is moreover through the most cursed country, and the Akasava are not a people that love long journeys save with the current of the river.

The silence was broken by the chief.

"Lord, we desire to put off our journey in your honour, for if we go, how shall we gather in palaver?"

Sanders shook his head.

"Let no man stop the hunter," quoth he. "Go in peace, chief, and you shall secure many teeth."[3] He saw a sudden light come to the chief's eyes, but continued, "I will send with you a sergeant of Houssas, that he may carry back to me the story of your prowess"—the light died away again—"for there will be many liars who will say that you never reached the Great Forest, and I shall have evidence to confound them."

Still the chief hesitated, and the waiting ranks listened, eagerly shuffling forward, till they ceased to bear any semblance to an ordered army, and were as a mob.

"Lord," said the chief, "we will go to-morrow——"

The smile was still on Sanders' lips, but his face was set, and his eyes held a steely glitter that the chief of the Akasava knew.

"You go to-day, my man," said Sanders, lowering his voice till he spoke in little more than a whisper, "else your warriors march under a new chief, and you swing on a tree."

"Lord, we go," said the man huskily, "though we are bad marchers and our feet are very tender."

Sanders, remembering the weariness of the Akasava, found his face twitching.

"With sore feet you may rest," he said significantly; "with sore backs you can neither march nor rest—go!"

At dawn the next morning the N'Gombi people came in twenty-five war canoes to join their Akasava friends, and found the village tenanted by women and old men, and Tigili, the king, in the shock of the discovery, surrendered quietly to the little party of Houssas on the beach.

"What comes to me, lord?" asked Tigili, the king.

Sanders whistled thoughtfully.

"I have some instructions about you somewhere," he said.

CHAPTER IX.
THE WOOD OF DEVILS.

Four days out of M'Sakidanga, if native report be true, there is a trickling stream that meanders down from N'Gombi country. Native report says that this is navigable even in the dry season.

The missionaries at Bonginda ridicule this report; and Arburt, the young chief of the station, with a gentle laugh in his blue eyes, listened one day to the report of Elebi about a fabulous land at the end of this river, and was kindly incredulous.

"If it be that ivory is stored in this place," he said in the vernacular, "or great wealth lies for the lifting, go to Sandi, for this ivory belongs to the Government. But do you, Elebi, fix your heart more upon God's treasures in heaven, and your thoughts upon your unworthiness to merit a place in His kingdom, and let the ivory go."

Elebi was known to Sanders as a native evangelist of the tornado type, a thunderous, voluble sub-minister of the service; he had, in his ecstatic moments, made many converts. But there were days of reaction, when Elebi sulked in his mud hut, and reviewed Christianity calmly.

It was a service, this new religion. You could not work yourself to a frenzy in it, and then have done with the thing for a week. You must needs go on, on, never tiring, never departing from the straight path, exercising irksome self-restraint, leaving undone that which you would rather do.

"Religion is prison," grumbled Elebi, after his interview, and shrugged his broad, black shoulders.

In his hut he was in the habit of discarding his European coat for the loin cloth and the blanket, for Elebi was a savage—an imitative savage—but still barbarian. Once, preaching on the River of Devils, he had worked himself up to such a pitch of enthusiastic fervour that he had smitten a scoffer, breaking his arm, and an outraged Sanders had him arrested, whipped, and fined a thousand rods. Hereafter Elebi had figured in certain English missionary circles as a Christian martyr, for he had lied magnificently, and his punishment had been represented as a form of savage persecution.

But the ivory lay buried three days' march beyond the Secret River; thus Elebi brooded over the log that smouldered in his hut day and night. Three days beyond the river, branching off at a place where there were two graves, the country was reputably full of devils, and Elebi shuddered at the thought; but, being a missionary and a lay evangelist, and, moreover, the proud possessor of a copy of the Epistle to the Romans (laboriously rendered into the native tongue), he had little to fear. He had more to fear from a certain White Devil at a far-away headquarters, who might be expected to range the lands of the Secret River, when the rains had come and gone.

It was supposed that Elebi had one wife, conforming to the custom of the white man, but the girl who came into the hut with a steaming bowl of fish in her hands was not the wife that the missionaries recognised as such.

"Sikini," he said, "I am going a journey by canoe."

"In the blessed service?" asked Sikini, who had come under the influence of the man in his more elated periods.

"The crackling of a fire is like a woman's tongue," quoted Elebi; "and it is easier to keep the lid on a boiling pot than a secret in a woman's heart."

Elebi had the river proverbs at his finger-tips, and the girl laughed, for she was his favourite wife, and knew that in course of time the information would come to her.

"Sikini," said the man suddenly, "you know that I have kept you when the Blood Taker would have me put you away."

(Arburt had a microscope and spent his evenings searching the blood of his flock for signs of trynosomiasis.)

"You know that for your sake I lied to him who is my father and my protector, saying: 'There shall be but one wife in my house, and that Tombolo, the coast woman.'"

The girl nodded, eyeing him stolidly.

"Therefore I tell you that I am going beyond the Secret River, three days' march, leaving the canoe at a place where there are two graves."

"What do you seek?" she asked.

"There are many teeth in that country," he said; "dead ivory that the people brought with them from a distant country, and have hidden, fearing one who is a Breaker of Stones.[4] I shall come back rich, and buy many wives who shall wait upon you and serve you, and then I will no longer be Christian, but will worship the red fetish as my father did, and his father."

"Go," she said, nodding thoughtfully.

He told her many things that he had not revealed to Arburt—of how the ivory came, of the people who guarded it, of the means by which he intended to secure it.

Next morning before the mission *lo-koli* sounded, he had slipped away in his canoe; and Arburt, when the news came to him, sighed and called him a disappointing beggar—for Arburt was human. Sanders, who was also human, sent swift messengers to arrest Elebi, for it is not a good thing that treasure-hunting natives should go wandering through a strange country, such excursions meaning war, and war meaning, to Sanders at any rate, solemn official correspondence, which his soul loathed.

Who would follow the fortunes of Elebi must paddle in his wake as far as Okau, where the Barina meets the Lapoi, must take the left river path, past the silent pool of the White Devil, must follow the winding stream till the elephants' playing ground be reached. Here the forest has been destroyed for the sport of the Great Ones; the shore is strewn with tree trunks, carelessly uprooted and as carelessly tossed aside by the gambolling mammoth. The ground is innocent of herbage or bush; it is a flat wallow of mud, with the marks of pads where the elephant has passed.

Elebi drew his canoe up the bank, carefully lifted his cooking-pot, full of living fire, and emptied its contents, heaping thereon fresh twigs and scraps of dead wood. Then he made himself a feast, and went to sleep.

A wandering panther came snuffling and howling in the night, and Elebi rose and replenished the fire. In the morning he sought for the creek that led to the Secret River, and found it hidden by the hippo grass.

Elebi had many friends in the N'Gombi country. They were gathered in the village of Tambango—to the infinite embarrassment of the chief of that village—for Elebi's friends laid hands upon whatsoever they desired, being strangers and well armed, and, moreover, outnumbering the men of the village three to one. One, O'Sako, did the chief hold in greatest dread, for he said little, but stalked tragically through the untidy street of Tambango, a bright, curved execution knife in the crook of his left arm. O'Sako was tall and handsome. One broad shoulder gleamed in its nakedness, and his muscular arms were devoid of ornamentation. His thick hair was plastered with clay till it was like a European woman's, and his body was smeared with ingola dust.

Once only he condescended to address his host.

"You shall find me three young men against the Lord Elebi's arrival, and they shall lead us to the land of the Secret River."

"But, master," pleaded the chief, "no man may go to the Secret River, because of the devils."

"Three men," said O'Sako softly; "three young men swift of foot, with eyes like the N'Gombi, and mouths silent as the dead."

"—— the devils," repeated the chief weakly, but O'Sako stared straight ahead and strode on.

When the sun blazed furiously on the rim of the world in a last expiring effort, and the broad river was a flood of fire, and long shadows ran through the clearings, Elebi came to the village. He came unattended from the south, and he brought with him no evidence of his temporary sojourn in the camps of civilisation. Save for his loin cloth, and his robe of panther skin thrown about his shoulders, he was naked.

There was a palaver house at the end of the village, a thatched little wattle hut perched on a tiny hill, and the Lord Elebi gathered there his captains and the chief of the village. He made a speech.

"*Cala, cala,*" he began—and it means "long ago," and is a famous opening to speeches—"before the white man came, and when the Arabi came down from the northern countries to steal women and ivory, the people of the Secret River buried their 'points' in a Place of Devils. Their women they could not bury, so they lost them. Now all the people of the Secret River are dead. The Arabi killed some, Bula Matadi killed others, but the sickness killed most of all. Where their villages were the high grass has grown, and in their gardens only the weaver bird speaks. Yet I know of this place, for there came to me a vision and a voice that said——"

The rest of the speech from the European standpoint was pure blasphemy, because Elebi had had the training of a lay preacher, and had an easy delivery.

When he had finished, the chief of the village of Tambangu spoke. It was a serious discourse on devils. There was no doubt at all that in the forest where the *caché* was there was a veritable stronghold of devildom. Some had bad faces and were as tall as the gum-trees—taller, for they used whole trees for clubs; some were small, so small that they travelled on the wings of bees, but all were very potent, very terrible, and most effective guardians of buried treasure. Their greatest accomplishment lay in leading astray the traveller: men went into the forest in search of game or copal or rubber, and never came back, because there were a thousand ways in and no way out.

Elebi listened gravely.

"Devils of course there are," he said, "including the Devil, the Old One, who is the enemy of God. I have had much to do with the casting out of devils—in my holy capacity as a servant of the Word. Of the lesser devils I know nothing, though I do not doubt they live. Therefore I think it would be better for all if we offered prayer."

On his instruction the party knelt in full view of the village, and Elebi prayed conventionally but with great earnestness that the Powers of Darkness should not prevail, but that the Great Work should go on triumphantly.

After which, to make doubly sure, the party sacrificed two fowls before a squat *bete* that stood before the chief's door, and a crazy witch-doctor anointed Elebi with human fat.

"We will go by way of Ochori," said Elebi, who was something of a strategist. "These Ochori folk will give us food and guides, being a cowardly folk and very fearful."

He took farewell of the old chief and continued his journey, with O'Sako and his warriors behind him. So two days passed. An hour's distance from the city of the Ochori he called a conference.

"Knowing the world," he said, "I am acquainted with the Ochori, who are slaves: you shall behold their chief embrace my feet. Since it is fitting that one, such as I, who know the ways of white men and their magic, should be received with honour; let us send forward a messenger to say that the Lord Elebi comes, and bid them kill so many goats against our coming."

"That is good talk," said O'Sako, his lieutenant, and a messenger was despatched.

Elebi with his caravan followed slowly.

It is said that Elebi's message came to Bosambo of Monrovia, chief of the Ochori, when he was in the despondent mood peculiar to men of action who find life running too smoothly.

It was Bosambo's practice—and one of which his people stood in some awe—to reflect aloud in English in all moments of crisis, or on any occasion when it was undesirable that his thoughts should be conveyed abroad.

He listened in silence, sitting before the door of his hut and smoking a short wooden pipe, whilst the messenger described the quality of the coming visitor, and the unparalleled honour which was to fall upon the Ochori.

Said Bosambo at the conclusion of the recital, "Damn nigger."

The messenger was puzzled by the strange tongue.

"Lord Chief," he said, "my master is a great one, knowing the ways of white men."

"I also know something of white men," said Bosambo calmly, in the River dialect, "having many friends, including Sandi, who married my brother's wife's sister, and is related to me. Also," said Bosambo daringly, "I have shaken hands with the Great White King who dwells beyond the big water, and he has given me many presents."

With this story the messenger went back to the slowly advancing caravan, and Elebi was impressed and a little bewildered.

"It is strange," he said, "no man has ever known an Ochori chief who was aught but a dog and the son of a dog—let us see this Bosambo. Did you tell him to come out and meet me?"

"No," replied the messenger frankly, "he was such a great one, and was so haughty because of Sandi, who married his brother's wife's sister; and so proud that I did not dare tell him."

There is a spot on the edge of the Ochori city where at one time Sanders had caused to be erected a warning sign, and here Elebi found the chief waiting and was flattered. There was a long and earnest conference in the little palaver house of the city, and here Elebi told as much of his story as was necessary, and Bosambo believed as much as he could.

"And what do you need of me and my people?" asked Bosambo at length.

"Lord chief," said Elebi, "I go a long journey, being fortified with the blessed spirit of which you know nothing, that being an especial mystery of the white men."

"There is no mystery which I did not know," said Bosambo loftily, "and if you speak of spirits, I will speak of certain saints, also of a Virgin who is held in high respect by white men."

"If you speak of the blessed Paul——" began Elebi, a little at sea.

"Not only of Paul but Peter, John, Luke, Matthew, Antonio, and Thomas," recited Bosambo rapidly. He had not been a scholar at the Catholic mission for nothing. Elebi was nonplussed.

"We will let these magic matters rest," said Elebi wisely; "it is evident to me that you are a learned man. Now I go to seek some wonderful treasures. All that I told you before was a lie. Let us speak as brothers. I go to the wood of devils, where no man has been for many years. I beg you, therefore, to give me food and ten men for carriers."

"Food you can have but no men," said Bosambo, "for I have pledged my word to Sandi, who is, as you know, the husband of my brother's wife's sister, that no man of mine should leave this country."

With this Elebi had to be content, for a new spirit had come to the Ochori since he had seen them last, and there was a defiance in the timid eyes of these slaves of other days which was disturbing. Besides, they seemed well armed.

In the morning the party set forth and Bosambo, who took no risks, saw them started on their journey. He observed that part of the equipment of the little caravan were two big baskets filled to the brim with narrow strips of red cloth.

"This is my magic," said Elebi mysteriously, when he was questioned, "it is fitting that you should know its power."

Bosambo yawned in his face with great insolence.

Clear of Ochori by one day's march, the party reached the first straggling advance guard of the Big Forest. A cloud of gum-trees formed the approach to the wood, and here the magic of Elebi's basket of cloth strips became revealed.

Every few hundred yards the party stopped, and Elebi tied one of the strips to a branch of a tree.

"In this way," he communicated to his lieutenant, "we may be independent of gods, and fearless of devils, for if we cannot find the ivory we can at least find our way back again."

(There had been such an experiment made by the missionaries in traversing the country between Bonguidga and the Big River, but there were no devils in that country.)

In two days' marches they came upon a place of graves. There had been a village there, for Isisi palms grew luxuriously, and pushing aside the grass they came upon a rotting roof. Also there were millions of weaver birds in the nut-palms, and a choked banana grove.

The graves, covered with broken cooking pots, Elebi found, and was satisfied.

In the forest, a league beyond the dead village, they came upon an old man, so old that you might have lifted him with a finger and thumb.

"Where do the young men go in their strength?" he mumbled childishly; "into the land of small devils? Who shall guide them back to their women? None, for the devils will confuse them, opening new roads and closing the old. Oh, Ko Ko!"

He snivelled miserably.

"Father," said Elebi, dangling strips of red flannel from his hand, "this is white man's magic, we come back by the way we go."

Then the old man fell into an insane fit of cursing, and threw at them a thousand deaths, and Elebi's followers huddled back in frowning fear.

"You have lived too long," said Elebi gently, and passed his spear through the old man's neck.

They found the ivory two days' journey beyond the place of killing. It was buried under a mound, which was overgrown with rank vegetation, and there was by European calculation some £50,000 worth.

"We will go back and find carriers," said Elebi, "taking with us as many of the teeth as we can carry."

Two hours later the party began its return journey, following the path where at intervals of every half-mile a strip of scarlet flannelette hung from a twig.

There were many paths they might have taken, paths that looked as though they had been made by the hand of man, and Elebi was glad that he had blazed the way to safety.

For eight hours the caravan moved swiftly, finding its direction with no difficulty; then the party halted for the night.

Elebi was awakened in the night by a man who was screaming, and he leapt up, stirring the fire to a blaze.

"It is the brother of Olambo of Kinshassa, he has the sickness *mongo*," said an awe-stricken voice, and Elebi called a council.

"There are many ways by which white men deal with this sickness," he said wisely, "by giving certain powders and by sticking needles into arms, but to give medicine for the sickness when madness comes is useless—so I have heard the fathers at the station say, because madness only comes when the man is near death."

"He was well last night," said a hushed voice. "There are many devils in the forest, let us ask him what he has seen."

So a deputation went to the screaming, writhing figure that lay trussed and tied on the ground, and spoke with him. They found some difficulty in gaining an opening, for he jabbered and mouthed and laughed and yelled incessantly.

"On the question of devils," at last Elebi said.

"Devils," screeched the madman. "Yi! I saw six devils with fire in their mouths—death to you, Elebi! Dog——"

He said other things which were not clean.

"If there were water here," mused Elebi, "we might drown him; since there is only the forest and the earth, carry him away from the camp, and I will make him silent."

So they carried the lunatic away, eight strong men swaying through the forest, and they came back, leaving Elebi alone with his patient. The cries ceased suddenly and Elebi returned, wiping his hands on his leopard skin.

"Let us sleep," said Elebi, and lay down.

Before the dawn came up the party were on the move.

They marched less than a mile from their camping ground and then faltered and stopped.

"There is no sign, lord," the leader reported, and Elebi called him a fool and went to investigate.

But there was no red flannel, not a sign of it. They went on another mile without success.

"We have taken the wrong path, let us return," said Elebi, and the party retraced its steps to the camp they had abandoned. That day was spent in exploring the country for three miles on either side, but there was no welcome blaze to show the trail.

"We are all N'Gombi men," said Elebi, "let us to-morrow go forward, keeping the sun at our back; the forest has no terrors for the N'Gombi folk—yet I cannot understand why the white man's magic failed."

"Devils!" muttered his lieutenant sullenly.

Elebi eyed him thoughtfully.

"Devils sometimes desire sacrifices," he said with significance, "the wise goat does not bleat when the priest approaches the herd."

In the morning a great discovery was made. A crumpled piece of flannel was found on the outskirts of the camp. It lay in the very centre of a path, and Elebi shouted in his joy.

Again the caravan started on the path. A mile farther along another little red patch caught his eye, half a mile beyond, another.

Yet none of these were where he had placed them, and they all bore evidence of rude handling, which puzzled the lay brother sorely. Sometimes the little rags would be missing altogether, but a search party would come upon one some distance off the track, and the march would go on.

Near sunset Elebi halted suddenly and pondered. Before him ran his long shadow; the sun was behind him when it ought to have been in front.

"We are going in the wrong direction," he said, and the men dropped their loads and stared at him.

"Beyond any doubt," said Elebi after a pause, "this is the work of devils—let us pray."

He prayed aloud earnestly for twenty minutes, and darkness had fallen before he had finished.

They camped that night on the spot where the last red guide was, and in the morning they returned the way they had come. There was plenty of provision, but water was hard to come by, and therein lay the danger. Less than a mile they had gone before the red rags had vanished completely, and they wandered helplessly in a circle.

"This is evidently a matter not for prayer, but for sacrifice," concluded Elebi, so they slew one of the guides.

Three nights later, O'Sako, the friend of Elebi, crawled stealthily to the place where Elebi was sleeping, and settled the dispute which had arisen during the day as to who was in command of the expedition.

"Master," said Bosambo of Monrovia, "all that you ordered me to do, that I did."

Sanders sat before the chief's hut in his camp chair and nodded.

"When your word came that I should find Elebi—he being an enemy of the Government and disobeying your word—I took fifty of my young men and followed on his tracks. At first the way was easy, because he had tied strips of cloth to the trees to guide him on the backward journey, but afterwards it was hard, for the *N'Kema* that live in the wood——"

"Monkeys?" Sanders raised his eyebrows.

"Monkeys, master," Bosambo nodded his head, "the little black monkeys of the forest who love bright colours—they had come down from their trees and torn away the cloths and taken them to their houses after the fashion of the monkey people. Thus Elebi lost himself and with him his men, for I found their bones, knowing the way of the forest."

"What else did you find?" asked Sanders.

"Nothing, master," said Bosambo, looking him straight in the eye.

"That is probably a lie!" said Sanders.

Bosambo thought of the ivory buried beneath the floor of his hut and did not contradict him.

CHAPTER X.
THE LOVES OF M'LINO.

When a man loves one woman, whether she be alive or dead, a deep and fragrant memory or a very pleasant reality, he is apt to earn the appellation of "woman-hater," a hasty judgment which the loose-minded pass upon any man whose loves lack promiscuosity, and who does not diffuse his passions. Sanders was described as a woman-hater by such men who knew him sufficiently little to analyse his character, but Sanders was not a woman-hater in any sense of the word, for he bore no illwill toward woman kind, and certainly was innocent of any secret love.

There was a young man named Ludley who had been assistant to Sanders for three months, at the end of which time Sanders sent for him—he was stationed at Isisi City.

"I think you can go home," said Sanders.

The young man opened his eyes in astonishment.

"Why?" he said.

Sanders made no reply, but stared through the open doorway at the distant village.

"Why?" demanded the young man again.

"I've heard things," said Sanders shortly—he was rather uncomfortable, but did not show it.

"Things—like what?"

Sanders shifted uneasily in his chair.

"Oh—things," he said vaguely, and added: "You go home and marry that nice girl you used to rave about when you first came out."

Young Ludley went red under his tan.

"Look here, chief!" he said, half angrily, half apologetically, "you're surely not going to take any notice—you know it's the sort of thing that's done in black countries—oh, damn it all, you're not going to act as censor over my morals, are you?"

Sanders looked at the youth coldly.

"Your morals aren't worth worrying about," he said truthfully. "You could be the most depraved devil in the world—which I'll admit you aren't—and I should not trouble to reform you. No. It's the morals of my cannibals that worry me. Home you go, my son; get married, *crescit sub pondere virtus*—you'll find the translation in the foreign phrase department of any respectable dictionary. As to the sort of things that are done in black countries, they don't do them in our black countries—monkey tricks of that sort are good enough for the Belgian Congo, or for Togoland, but they aren't good enough for this little strip of wilderness."

Ludley went home.

He did not tell anybody the real reason why he had come home, because it would not have sounded nice. He was a fairly decent boy, as boys of his type go, and he said nothing worse about Sanders than that he was a woman-hater.

The scene that followed his departure shows how little the white mind differs from the black in its process of working. For, after seeing his assistant safely embarked on a homeward-bound boat, Sanders went up the river to Isisi, and there saw a woman who was called M'Lino.

The average black woman is ugly of face, but beautiful of figure, but M'Lino was no ordinary woman, as you shall learn. The Isisi people, who keep extraordinary records in their heads, the information being handed from father to son, say that M'Lino came from an Arabi family, and certainly if a delicately-chiselled nose, a refinement of lip, prove anything, they prove M'Lino came from no pure Bantu stock.

She came to Sanders when he sent for her, alert, suspicious, very much on her guard.

Before he could speak, she asked him a question.

"Lord, where is Lijingii?" This was the nearest the native ever got to the pronunciation of Ludley's name.

"Lijingii has gone across the black water," said Sanders gently, "to his own people."

"You sent him, lord," she said quickly, and Sanders made no reply.

"Lord," she went on, and Sanders wondered at the bitterness in her tone, "it is said that you hate women."

"Then a lie is told," said Sanders. "I do not hate women; rather I greatly honour them, for they go down to the caves of hell when they bear children; also I regard them highly because they are otherwise brave and very loyal."

She said nothing. Her head was sunk till her chin rested on her bare, brown breast, but she looked at him from under her brows, and her eyes were filled with a strange luminosity. Something like a panic awoke in Sanders' heart—had the mischief been done? He cursed Ludley, and breathed a fervent, if malevolent, prayer that his ship would go down with him. But her words reassured him.

"I made Lijingii love me," she said, "though he was a great lord, and I was a slave; I also would have gone down to hell, for some day I hoped I should bear him children, but now that can never be."

"And thank the Lord for it!" said Sanders, under his breath.

He would have given her some words of cheer, but she turned abruptly from him and walked away. Sanders watched the graceful figure as it receded down the straggling street, and went back to his steamer.

He was ten miles down the river before he remembered that the reproof he had framed for the girl had been undelivered.

"That is very extraordinary," said Sanders, with some annoyance, "I must be losing my memory."

Three months later young Penson came out from England to take the place of the returned Ludley. He was a fresh-faced youth, bubbling over with enthusiasm, and, what is more important, he had served a two-years' apprenticeship at Sierra Leone.

"You are to go up to Isisi," said Sanders, "and I want to tell you that you've got to be jolly careful."

"What's the racket?" demanded the youth eagerly. "Are the beggars rising?"

"So far as I know," said Sanders, putting his feet up on the rail of the verandah, "they are not—it is not bloodshed, but love that you've got to guard against."

And he told the story of M'Lino, even though it was no creditable story to British administration.

"You can trust me," said young Penson, when he had finished.

"I trust you all right," said Sanders, "but I don't trust the woman—let me hear from you from time to time; if you don't write about her I shall get suspicious, and I'll come along in a very unpleasant mood."

"You can trust me," said young Penson again; for he was at the age when a man is very sure of himself.

Remarkable as it may read, from the moment he left to take up his new post until he returned to headquarters, in disgrace, a few months later, he wrote no word of the straight, slim girl, with her wonderful eyes. Other communications came to hand, official reports, terse and to the point, but no mention of M'Lino, and Sanders began to worry.

The stories came filtering through, extraordinary stories of people who had been punished unjustly, of savage floggings administered by order of the sub-commissioner, and Sanders took boat and travelled up the river *hec dum*.

He landed short of the town, and walked along the river bank. It was not an easy walk, because the country hereabouts is a riot of vegetation. Then he came upon an African idyll—a young man, who sat playing on a squeaky violin, for the pleasure of M'Lino, lying face downwards on the grass, her chin in her hands.

"In the name of a thousand devils!" said Sanders wrathfully; and the boy got up from the fallen tree on which he sat, and looked at him calmly, and with no apparent embarrassment. Sanders looked down at the girl and pointed.

"Go back to the village, my woman," he said softly, for he was in a rage.

"Now, you magnificent specimen of a white man," he said, when the girl had gone—slowly and reluctantly—"what is this story I hear about your flogging O'Sako?"

The youth took his pipe from his pocket and lit it coolly.

"He beat M'Lino," he said, in the tone of one who offered full justification.

"From which fact I gather that he is the unfortunate husband of that attractive nigger lady you were charming just now when I arrived?"

"Don't be beastly," said the other, scowling. "I know she's a native and all that sort of thing, but my people at home will get used to her colour——"

"Go on board my boat," said Sanders quietly. "Regard yourself as my prisoner."

Sanders brought him down to headquarters without troubling to investigate the flogging of O'Sako, and no word passed concerning M'Lino till they were back again at headquarters.

"Of course I shall send you home," said Sanders.

"I supposed you would," said the other listlessly. He had lost all his self-assurance on the journey down river, and was a very depressed young man indeed.

"I must have been mad," he admitted, the day before the mail boat called *en route* for England; "from the very first I loved her—good heavens, what an ass I am!"

"You are," agreed Sanders, and saw him off to the ship with a cheerful heart.

"I will have no more sub-commissioners at Isisi," he wrote acidly to the Administration. "I find my work sufficiently entertaining without the additional amusement of having to act as chaperon to British officials."

He made a special journey to Isisi to straighten matters out, and M'Lino came unbidden to see him.

"Lord, is he gone, too?" she asked.

"When I want you, M'Lino," said Sanders, "I will send for you."

"I loved him," she said, with more feeling than Sanders thought was possible for a native to show.

"You are an easy lover," said Sanders.

She nodded.

"That is the way with some women," she said. "When I love, I love with terrible strength; when I hate, I hate for ever and ever—I hate you, master!"

She said it very simply.

"If you were a man," said the exasperated Commissioner, "I would tie you up and whip you."

"F—f—b!" said the girl contemptuously, and left him staring.

To appreciate the position, you have to realise that Sanders was lord of all this district; that he had the power of life and death, and no man dared question or disobey his word. Had M'Lino been a man, as he said, she would have suffered for her treason—there is no better word for her offence—but she was a woman, and a seriously gifted woman, and, moreover, sure of whatever powers she had.

He did not see her again during the three days he was in the city, nor (this is the extraordinary circumstance) did he discuss her with the chief. He learned that she had become the favourite wife of O'Sako; that she had many lovers and scorned her husband, but he sought no news of her. Once he saw her walking towards him, and went out of his way to avoid her. It was horribly weak and he knew it, but he had no power to resist the impulse that came over him to give her a wide berth.

Following this visit, Sanders was coming down stream at a leisurely pace, he himself at the steering wheel, and his eyes searching the treacherous river for sand banks. His mind was filled with the problem of M'Lino, when suddenly in the bush that fringes the Isisi river, something went "woof," and the air was filled with flying potlegs. One struck his cabin, and splintered a panel to shreds, many fell upon the water, one missed Sergeant Abiboo's head and sent his *tarbosh* flying.

Sanders rang his engines astern, being curious to discover what induced the would-be assassin to fire a blunderbuss in his direction, and Abiboo, bare-headed, went pattering forward and slipped the canvas cover from the gleaming little Maxim.

Then four Houssa soldiers jumped into the water and waded ashore, holding their rifles above their heads with the one hand and their ammunition in the other, and Sanders stood by the rail of the boat, balancing a sporting Lee-Enfield in the crook of his arm.

Whoever fired the shot had chosen the place of killing very well. The bush was very thick, the approach to land lay through coarse grass that sprang from the swamp, vegetation ran rank, and a tangle of creeper formed a screen that would have been impenetrable to a white man.

But the Houssas had a way—they found the man with his smoking gun, waiting calmly.

He was of the Isisi people—a nation of philosophers—and he surrendered his weapon without embarrassment.

"I think," he said to Sergeant Abiboo, as they hurried down the bank to the river-side, "this means death."

"Death and the torments of hell to follow," said Abiboo, who was embittered by the loss of his *tarbosh*, which had cost him five francs in the French territory.

Sanders put up his rifle when he saw the prisoner. He held an informal court in the shattered deck cabin.

"Did you shoot at me?" he asked.

"I did, master," said the man.

"Why?"

"Because," the prisoner replied, "you are a devil and exercise witchcraft."

Sanders was puzzled a little.

"In what particular section of the devil department have I been busy?" he asked in the vernacular.

The prisoner was gazing at him steadily.

"Master," he replied, "it is not my business to understand these things. It is said to me, 'kill'—and I kill."

Sanders wasted no more time in vain questions. The man was put in irons, the nose of the steamer turned again down stream, and the Commissioner resumed his vigil.

Midway between B'Fani and Lakaloli he came to a tying-up place. Here there were dead trees for the chopping, and he put his men to replenish his stock of fuel.

He was annoyed, not because a man had attempted to take his life, nor even because his neat little cabin forward was a litter of splinters and broken glass where the potleg had struck, but because he nosed trouble where he thought all was peace and harmony.

He had control of some sixteen distinct and separate nations, each isolated and separated from the other by custom and language. They were distinct, not as the French are from the Italian, but as the Slav is from the Turk.

In the good old times before the English came there were many wars, tribe against tribe, people against people. There were battles, murders, raidings, and wholesale crucifixions, but the British changed all that. There was peace in the land.

Sanders selected with care a long, thin cigar from his case, nibbled at the end and lit it.

The prisoner sat on the steel deck of the *Zaire* near the men's quarters. He was chained by the leg-iron to a staple, and did not seem depressed to any extent. When Sanders made his appearance, a camp stool in his hand, the Commissioner seated himself, and began his inquisition.

"How do they call you, my man?"

"Bofabi of Isisi."

"Who told you to kill me?"

"Lord, I forget."

"A man or a woman?"

"Lord, it may have been either."

More than that Sanders could not learn, and the subsequent examination at Isisi taught Sanders nothing, for, when confronted with M'Lino, the man said that he did not know her.

Sanders went back to his base in a puzzled frame of mind, and Bofabi of Isisi was sent to the convict establishment at the river's mouth. There matters stood for three months, and all that Sanders learnt of the girl was that she had a new lover whose name was Tebeki, and who was chief of the Akasava.

There were three months of peace and calm, and then Tebeki, coveting his neighbour's wife, took three hundred spears down into the Isisi country, burnt the village that sheltered her, crucified her husband, and carried her back with him.

In honour of this achievement Tebeki gave a feast and a beer dance. There were great and shameless orgies that lasted five days, and the strip of forest that fringes the river between the Isisi and the lower river became a little inferno.

At the end of the five days Tebeki sat down to consider his position. He was in the act of inventing justification for his crime, when Sanders came on the scene. More ominous were the ten Houssas and the Maxim which accompanied the brown-faced little man.

Sanders walked to Tebeki's hut and called him out, and Tebeki, blear-eyed and shaky, stepped forth into the hot sunshine, blinking.

"Tebeki," said Sanders, "what of O'Sako and his village?"

"Master," said Tebeki, slowly, "he put shame upon me——"

"Spare me your lies," said Sanders coldly, and signed to the Houssas.

Then he looked round for a suitable tree. There was one behind the hut—a great copal-gum.

"In half an hour I shall hang you," said Sanders, looking at his watch.

Tebeki said nothing; only his bare feet fidgeted in the dust.

There came out of the hut a tall girl, who stood eyeing the group with curiosity; then she came forward, and laid her hand on Tebeki's bare shoulder.

"What will you do with my man?" she asked. "I am M'Lino, the wife of O'Sako."

Sanders was not horrified, he showed his teeth in a mirthless grin and looked at her.

"You will find another man, M'Lino," he said, "as readily as you found this one." Then he turned away to give directions for the hanging. But the woman followed him, and boldly laid her hand on his arm.

"Master," she said, "if any was wronged by O'Sako's death, was it not I, his wife? Yet I say let Tebeki go free, for I love him."

"You may go to the devil," said Sanders politely; "I am getting tired of you and your lovers."

He hanged Tebeki, expeditiously and with science, and the man died immediately, because Sanders was very thorough in this sort of business. Then he and the Houssa corps marched away, and the death song of the woman sounded fainter and fainter as the forest enveloped him. He camped that night on the Hill of Trees, overlooking the sweeping bend of the river, and in the morning his orderly came to tell him that the wife of O'Sako desired to see him.

Sanders cursed the wife of O'Sako, but saw her.

She opened her mission without preliminary.

"Because of the death I brought to O'Sako, my husband, and Tebeki, my lover, the people have cast me forth," she said. "Every hand is against me, and if I stay in this country I shall die."

"Well?" said Sanders.

"So I will go with you, until you reach the Sangar River, which leads to the Congo. I have brothers there."

"All this may be true," said Sanders dispassionately; "on the other hand, I know that your heart is filled with hate because I have taken two men from you, and hanged a third. Nevertheless, you shall come with us as far as the Sangar River, but you shall not touch the 'chop' of my men, nor shall you speak with them."

She nodded and left him, and Sanders issued orders for her treatment.

In the middle of the night Abiboo, who, in addition to being Sanders' servant, was a sergeant of the Houssas, came to Sanders' tent, and the Commissioner jumped out of bed and mechanically reached for his Express.

"Leopards?" he asked briefly.

"Master," said Sergeant Abiboo, "it is the woman M'Lino—she is a witch."

"Sergeant," said the exasperated Sanders, "if you wake me up in the middle of the night with that sort of talk, I will break your infernal head."

"Be that as it may, master," said the sergeant stolidly, "she is a witch, for she has talked with my men and done many wonderful things—such as causing them to behold their children and far-away scenes."

"Have I an escort of babies?" asked Sanders despairingly. "I wish," he went on, with quiet savageness, "I had chosen Kroomen or Bushmen"—the sergeant winced—"or the mad people of the Isisi River, before I took a half-company of the King's Houssas."

The sergeant gulped down the insult, saying nothing.

"Bring the woman to me," said Sanders. He scrambled into his clothing, and lit his tent lantern.

After a while he heard the pattering of bare feet, and the girl came into his tent, and regarded him quietly.

"M'Lino," said Sanders, "I told you that you were not to speak with my men."

"Lord," she said, "they spoke with me first."

"Is this true?"

The sergeant at the tent door nodded. "Tembeli, the son of Sekambano, spoke with her, thus disobeying orders, and the other men followed," he said.

"Bushmen by gad!" fumed Sanders. "You will take Tembeli, the son of Sekambano, tie him to a tree, and give him twenty lashes."

The sergeant saluted, produced a tawdry little notebook, all brass binding and gold edges, and made a laborious note.

"As for you," said Sanders to the woman, "you drop your damned bush-mesmerism, or I'll treat you in the same way—*alaki*?"

"Yes, lord," she said meekly, and departed.

Two Houssas tied Tembeli to a tree, and the sergeant gave him twenty-one with a pliable hippo-hide—the extra one being the sergeant's perquisite.

In the morning the sergeant reported that Tembeli had died in the night, and Sanders worried horribly.

"It isn't the flogging," he said; "he has had the *chicotte* before."

"It is the woman," said the sergeant wisely. "She is a witch; I foresaw this when she joined the column."

They buried Tembeli, the son of Sekambano, and Sanders wrote three reports of the circumstances of the death, each of which he tore up.

Then he marched on.

That night the column halted near a village, and Sanders sent the woman, under escort, to the chief, with orders to see her safely to the Sangar River. In half an hour she returned, with the escort, and Sergeant Abiboo explained the circumstances.

"The chief will not take her in, being afraid."

"Afraid?" Sanders spluttered in his wrath; "Afraid? What is he afraid of?"

"Her devilry," said the sergeant; "the *lo-koli* has told him the story of Tebeki, and he will not have her."

Sanders swore volubly for five minutes; then he went off to interview the chief of the village.

The interview was short and to the point. Sanders knew this native very well, and made no mistakes.

"Chief," he said at the end of the palaver, "two things I may do; one is to punish you for your disobedience, and the other is to go on my way."

"Master," said the other earnestly, "if you give my village to the fire, yet I would not take the woman M'Lino."

"So much I realise," said Sanders; "therefore I will go on my way."

He marched at dawn on the following day, the woman a little ahead of the column, and under his eye. Halting for a "chop" and rest at mid-day, a man of the Houssas came to him and said there was a dead man hanging from a tree in the wood. Sanders went immediately with the man to the place of the hanging, for he was responsible for the peace of the district.

"Where?" he asked, and the man pointed to a straight gum-tree that stood by itself in a clearing.

"Where?" asked Sanders again, for there was no evidence of tragedy. The man still pointed at the tree, and Sanders frowned.

"Go forward and touch his foot," said the Commissioner, and, after a little hesitation, the soldier walked slowly to the tree and put out his hand. But he touched nothing but air, as far as Sanders could see.

"You are mad," he said, and whistled for the sergeant.

"What do you see there?" asked Sanders, and the sergeant replied instantly:

"Beyond the hanging man——"

"There is no hanging man," said Sanders coolly—for he began to appreciate the need for calm reasoning—"nothing but a tree and some shadows."

The Houssa looked puzzled, and turned a grave face to his.

"Master, there is a man hanging," he said.

"That is so," said Sanders quietly; "we must investigate this matter." And he signed for the party to return to the camp.

On the way he asked carelessly if the sergeant had spoken with the woman M'Lino.

"I saw her, but she did not speak, except with her eyes."

Sanders nodded. "Tell me," he said, "where did you bury Tembeli, the son of Sekambano?"

"Master, we left him, in accordance with our custom, on the ground at the foot of a tree."

Sanders nodded again, for this is not the custom of the Houssas.

"We will go back on our tracks to the camping place where the woman came to us," he said.

They marched until sundown, and whilst two men pitched his tent Sanders strolled round the little camp. The men were sitting about their cooking-pots, but the woman M'Lino sat apart, her elbows on her knees, her face between her hands.

"M'Lino," he said to her, halting suddenly before her, "how many men have you killed in your life?"

She looked at him long and fixedly, and he returned the stare; then she dropped her eyes. "Many men," she said.

"So I think," said Sanders.

He was eating his dinner when Abiboo came slowly toward him.

"Master, the man has died," he said.

Sanders looked at him narrowly.

"Which man?"

"The man you chicotted with your own hand," said Abiboo.

Now, the Commissioner had neither chicotted a man, nor had he ordered punishment, but he replied in a matter-of-fact tone, "I will see him."

113

On the edge of the camp there was a little group about a prostrate figure. The Houssas fell apart with black looks as Sanders came near, and there was some muttering. Though Sanders did not see it, M'Lino looked strangely at Ahmid, a Houssa, who took up his rifle and went stealthily into the bush.

The Commissioner bent over the man who lay there, felt his breast, and detected no beat of heart.

"Get me my medicine chest," he said, but none obeyed him.

"Sergeant," he repeated, "bring my medicine chest!"

Abiboo saluted slowly, and, with every appearance of reluctance, went.

He came back with the case of undressed skin, and Sanders opened it, took out the ammonia bottle, and applied it to the man's nose. He made no sign.

"We shall see," was all that Sanders said when the experiment failed. He took a hypodermic syringe and filled the little tube with a solution of strychnine. This he jabbed unceremoniously into the patient's back. In a minute the corpse sat up, jerkily.

"Ha!" said Sanders, cheerfully; "I am evidently a great magician!"

He rose to his feet, dusted his knees, and beckoned the sergeant.

"Take four men and return to the place where you left Tembeli. If the leopards have not taken him, you will meet him on the road, because by this time he will have waked up."

He saw the party march off, then turned his attention to M'Lino.

"My woman," he said, "it is evident to me that you are a witch, although I have met your like before"—it was observed that the face of Sanders was very white. "I cannot flog you, because you are a woman, but I can kill you."

She laughed.

Their eyes met in a struggle for mastery, and so they stared at one another for a space of time which seemed to Sanders a thousand years, but which was in all probability less than a minute.

"It would be better if you killed yourself," she said.

"I think so," said Sanders dully, and fumbled for his revolver.

It was half drawn, his thumb on the hammer, when a rifle banged in the bushes and the woman fell forward without a word.

Ahmid, the Houssa, was ever a bad shot.

"I believe," said Sanders, later, "that you took your rifle to kill me, being under the influence of M'Lino, so I will make no bad report against you."

"Master," said the Houssa simply, "I know nothing of the matter."

"That I can well believe," said Sanders, and gave the order to march.

CHAPTER XI.
THE WITCH-DOCTOR.

Nothing surprised Sanders except the ignorance of the average stay-at-home Briton on all matters pertaining to the savage peoples of Africa. Queer things happened in the "black patch"—so the coast officials called Sanders' territory—miraculous, mysterious things, but Sanders was never surprised. He had dealings with folks who believed in ghosts and personal devils, and he sympathised with them, realising that it is very difficult to ascribe all the evils of life to human agencies.

Sanders was an unquiet man, or so his constituents thought him, and a little mad; this also was the native view. Worst of all, there was no method in his madness.

Other commissioners might be depended upon to arrive after the rains, sending word ahead of their coming. This was a good way—the Isisi, the Ochori, and the N'Gombi people, everlastingly at issue, were agreed upon this—because, with timely warning of the Commissioner's approach, it was possible to thrust out of sight the ugly evidence of fault, to clean up and make tidy the muddle of folly.

It was bad to step sheepishly forth from your hut into the clear light of the rising sun, with all the débris of an overnight feast mutely testifying to your discredit, and face the cold, unwavering eyes of a little brown-faced man in immaculate white. The switch he carried in his hand would be smacking his leg suggestively, and there were always four Houssa soldiers in blue and scarlet in the background, immobile, but alert, quick to obey.

Once Sanders came to a N'Gombi village at dawn, when by every known convention he should have been resting in his comfortable bungalow some three hundred miles down river.

Sanders came strolling through the village street just as the sun topped the trees and long shadows ran along the ground before the flood of lemon-coloured light.

The village was silent and deserted, which was a bad sign, and spoke of overnight orgies. Sanders walked on until he came to the big square near the palaver house, and there the black ruin of a dead fire smoked sullenly.

Sanders saw something that made him go raking amongst the embers.

"Pah!" said Sanders, with a wry face.

He sent back to the steamer for the full force of his Houssa guard, then he walked into the chief's hut and kicked him till he woke.

He came out blinking and shivering, though the morning was warm.

"Telemi, son of O'ari," said Sanders, "tell me why I should not hang you—man-eater and beast."

"Lord," said the chief, "we chopped this man because he was an enemy, stealing into the village at night, and carrying away our goats and our dogs. Besides which, we did not know that you were near by."

"I can believe that," said Sanders.

A *lo-koli* beat the villages to wakefulness, and before a silent assembly the headman of the N'Gombi village was scientifically flogged.

Then Sanders called the elders together and said a few words of cheer and comfort.

"Only hyenas and crocodiles eat their kind," he said, "also certain fishes." (There was a general shudder, for amongst the N'Gombi to be likened to a fish is a deadly insult.) "Cannibals I do not like, and they are hated by the King's Government. Therefore when it comes to my ears—and I have many spies—that you chop man, whether he be enemy or friend, I will come quickly and I will flog sorely; and if it should again happen I will bring with me a rope, and I will find me a tree, and there will be broken huts in this land."

Again they shuddered at the threat of the broken hut, for it is the custom of the N'Gombi to break down the walls of a dead man's house to give his spirit free egress.

Sanders carried away with him the chief of the village, with leg-irons at his ankles, and in course of time the prisoner arrived at a little labour colony on the coast, where he worked for five years in company with other indiscreet headmen who were suffering servitude for divers offences.

They called Sanders in the Upper River districts by a long and sonorous name, which may be euphemistically translated as "The man who has a faithless wife," the little joke of Bosambo, chief of the Ochori, and mightily subtle because Sanders was wedded to his people.

North and south, east and west, he prowled. He travelled by night and by day. Sometimes his steamer would go threshing away up river, and be watched out of sight by the evil-doing little fishing-villages.

"Go you," said Sarala, who was a little headman of the Akasava, "go you three hours' journey in your canoe and watch the river for Sandi's return. And at first sign of his steamer—which you may see if you climb the hill at the river's bend—come back and warn me, for I desire to follow certain customs of my father in which Sandi has no pleasure."

He spoke to two of his young men and they departed. That night by the light of a fire, to the accompaniment of dancing and drum-beating, the son of the headman brought his firstborn, ten hours old, squealing noisily, as if with knowledge of the doom ahead, and laid it at his father's feet.

"People," said the little chief, "it is a wise saying of all, and has been a wise saying since time began, that the firstborn has a special virtue; so that if we sacrifice him to sundry gods and devils, good luck will follow us in all our doings."

He said a word to the son, who took a broad-bladed spear and began turning the earth until he had dug a little grave. Into this, alive, the child was laid, his little feet kicking feebly against the loose mould.

"Oh, gods and devils," invoked the old man, "we shed no blood, that this child may come to you unblemished."

The son stirred a heap of loose earth with his foot, so that it fell over the baby's legs; then into the light of the fire stepped Sanders, and the chief's son fell back.

Sanders was smoking a thin cigar, and he smoked for fully a minute without saying a word, and a minute was a very long time. Then he stepped to the grave, stooped, and lifted the baby up awkwardly, for he was more used to handling men than babes, gave it a little shake to clear it of earth, and handed it to a woman.

"Take the child to its mother," he said, "and tell her to send it to me alive in the morning, otherwise she had best find a new husband."

Then he turned to the old chief and his son.

"Old man," he said, "how many years have you to live?"

"Master," said the old man, "that is for you to say."

Sanders scratched his chin reflectively, and the old man watched him with fear in his eyes.

"You will go to Bosambo, chief of the Ochori, telling him I have sent you, and you shall till his garden, and carry his water until you die," said Sanders.

"I am so old that that will be soon," said the old man.

"If you were younger it would be sooner," said Sanders. "As for your son, we will wait until the morning."

The Houssas in the background marched the younger man to the camp Sanders had formed down river—the boat that had passed had been intended to deceive a chief under suspicion—and in the morning, when the news came that the child was dead—whether from shock, or injury, or exposure, Sanders did not trouble to inquire—the son of the chief was hanged.

I tell these stories of Sanders of the River, that you may grasp the type of man he was and learn something of the work he had to do. If he was quick to punish, he acted in accordance with the spirit of the people he governed, for they had no memory; and yesterday, with its faults, its errors and its teachings, was a very long time ago, and a man resents an unjust punishment for a crime he has forgotten.

It is possible to make a bad mistake, but Sanders never made one, though he was near to doing so once.

Sanders was explaining his point of view in regard to natives to Professor Sir George Carsley, when that eminent scientist arrived unexpectedly at headquarters, having been sent out by the British Government to study tropical disease at first hand.

Sir George was a man of some age, with a face of exceptional pallor and a beard that was snowy white.

"There was a newspaper man who said I treated my people like dogs," said Sanders slowly, for he was speaking in English, a language that was seldom called for. "I believe I do. That is to say, I treat them as if they were real good dogs, not to be petted one minute and kicked the next; not to be encouraged to lie on the drawing-room mat one day, and the next cuffed away from the dining-room hearthrug."

Sir George made no answer. He was a silent man, who had had some experience on the coast, and had lived for years in the solitude of a Central African province, studying the habits of the malarial mosquito.

Sanders was never a great conversationalist, and the three days the professor spent at headquarters were deadly dull ones for the Commissioner.

On one subject alone did the professor grow talkative.

"I want to study the witch-doctor," he said. "I think there is no appointment in the world that would give me a greater sense of power than my appointment by a native people to that post."

Sanders thought the scientist was joking, but the other returned to the subject again and again, gravely, earnestly, and persistently, and for his entertainment Sanders recited all the stories he had ever heard of witch-doctors and their tribe.

"But you don't expect to learn anything from these people?" said Sanders, half in joke.

"On the contrary," said the professor, seriously; "I anticipate making valuable scientific discoveries through my intercourse with them."

"Then you're a silly old ass," said Sanders; but he said it to himself.

The pale professor left him at the end of the fourth day, and beyond an official notification that he had established himself on the border, no further news came of the scientist for six months, until one evening came the news that the pale-faced old man had been drowned by the upsetting of a canoe. He had gone out on a solitary excursion, taking with him some scientific apparatus, and nothing more was heard of him until his birch-bark canoe was discovered, bottom up, floating on the river.

No trace of Sir George was found, and in the course of time Sanders collected the dead man's belongings and forwarded them to England.

There were two remarkable facts about this tragedy, the first being that Sanders found no evidence either in papers or diaries, of the results of any scientific research work performed by the professor other than a small note-book. The second was, that in his little book the scientist had carefully recorded the stories Sanders had told him of witch doctors.

(Sanders recognised at least one story which he had himself invented on the spur of the moment for the professor's entertainment.)

Six more or less peaceful months passed, and then began the series of events which make up the story of the Devil Man.

It began on the Little River.

There was a woman of the Isisi people who hated her husband, though he was very good to her, building her a hut and placing an older wife to wait upon her.

He gave her many presents, including a great neck-ring of brass, weighing pounds, that made her the most envied woman on the Isisi River. But her hatred for her husband was unquenched; and one morning she came out from her hut, looking dazed and frightened, and began in a quavering voice to sing the Song of the Dead, mechanically pouring little handfuls of dust on her head, and the villagers went in, to find the man stark and staring, with a twisted grin on his dead face and the pains of hell in his eyes.

In the course of two days they burned the husband in the Middle River; and as the canoe bearing the body swept out of sight round a bend of the river, the woman stepped into the water and laved the dust from her grimy body and stripped the green leaves of mourning from her waist.

Then she walked back to the village with a light step, for the man she hated best was dead and there was an end to it.

Four days later came Sanders, a grim little man, with a thin, brown face and hair inclined to redness.

"M'Fasa," he said, standing at the door of her hut and looking down at her, as with a dogged simulation of indifference she pounded her grain, "they tell me your man has died."

"Lord, that is true," she said. "He died of a sudden sickness."

"Too sudden for my liking," said Sanders, and disappeared into the dark interior of the hut. By and by Sanders came back into the light and looked down on her. In his hand was a tiny glass phial, such as Europeans know very well, but which was a remarkable find in a heathen village.

"I have a fetish," he said, "and my fetish has told me that you poisoned your husband, M'Fasa."

"Your fetish lies," she said, not looking up.

"I will not argue that matter," said Sanders wisely, for he had no proofs beyond his suspicions; and straightway he summoned to him the chief man of the village.

There was a little wait, the woman pounding her corn slowly, with downcast eyes, pausing now and then to wipe the sweat from her forehead with the back of her hand, and Sanders, his helmet on the back of his head, a half-smoked cheroot in his mouth, hands thrust deep into his duck-pockets and an annoyed frown on his face, looking at her.

By and by came the chief tardily, having been delayed by the search for a soldier's scarlet coat, such as he wore on great occasions.

"Master, you sent for me," he said.

Sanders shifted his gaze.

"On second thoughts," he said, "I do not need you."

The chief went away with a whole thanksgiving service in his heart, for there had been certain secret doings on the river for which he expected reprimand.

"M'Fasa, you will go to my boat," said Sanders, and the woman, putting down her mortar, rose and went obediently to the steamer. Sanders followed slowly, having a great many matters to consider. If he denounced this woman to the elders of the village, she would be stoned to death; if he carried her to headquarters and tried her, there was no evidence on which a conviction might be secured. There was no place to which he could deport her, yet to leave her would be to open the way for further mischief.

She awaited him on the deck of the *Zaire*, a straight, shapely girl of eighteen, fearless, defiant.

"M'Fasa," said Sanders, "why did you kill your husband?"

"Lord, I did not kill him; he died of the sickness," she said, as doggedly as before.

Sanders paced the narrow deck, his head on his breast, for this was a profound problem. Then he looked up.

"You may go," he said; and the woman, a little puzzled, walked along the plank that connected the boat with the shore, and disappeared into the bush.

Three weeks later his spies brought word that men were dying unaccountably on the Upper River. None knew why they died, for a man would sit down strong and full of cheer to his evening meal, and lo! in the morning, when his people went to wake him, he would be beyond waking, being most unpleasantly dead.

This happened in many villages on the Little River.

"It's getting monotonous," said Sanders to the captain of the Houssas. "There is some wholesale poisoning going on, and I am going up to find the gentleman who dispenses the dope."

It so happened that the first case claiming investigation was at Isisi City. It was a woman who had died, and this time Sanders suspected the husband, a notorious evil-doer.

"Okali," he said, coming to the point, "why did you poison your wife?"

121

"Lord," said the man, "she died of the sickness. In the evening she was well, but at the dark hour before sun came she turned in her sleep saying 'Ah! oh!' and straightway she died."

Sanders drew a long breath.

"Get a rope," he said to one of his men, and when the rope arrived Abiboo scrambled up to the lower branch of a copal-gum and scientifically lashed a block and tackle.

"Okali," said Sanders, "I am going to hang you for the murder of your wife, for I am a busy man and have no time to make inquiries; and if you are not guilty of her murder, yet there are many other abominable deeds you have been guilty of, therefore I am justified in hanging you."

The man was grey with terror when they slipped the noose over his neck and strapped his hands behind him.

"Lord, she was a bad wife to me and had many lovers," he stammered. "I did not mean to kill her, but the Devil Man said that such medicine would make her forget her lovers——"

"Devil Man! What Devil Man?" asked Sanders quickly.

"Lord, there is a devil greatly respected in these parts, who wanders in the forest all the time and gives many curious medicines."

"Where is he to be found?"

"Lord, none know. He comes and goes, like a grey ghost, and he has a fetish more powerful than a thousand ordinary devils. Master, I gave the woman, my wife, that which he gave to me, and she died. How might I know that she would die?"

"*Cheg'li*," said Sanders shortly to the men at the rope-end, and *cheg'li* in the dialect of the River means "pull."

"Stop!"

Sanders was in a changeable mood, and a little irritable by reason of the fact that he knew himself to be fickle.

"How came this drug to you? In powder, in liquid, or——"

The man's lips were dry. He could do no more than shake his head helplessly.

"Release him," said Sanders; and Abiboo loosened the noose and unstrapped the man's hands.

"If you have lied to me," said Sanders, "you die at sunset. First let me hear more of this Devil Man, for I am anxious to make his acquaintance."

He gave the man ten minutes to recover from the effects of his fear, then sent for him.

"Lord," said he, "I know nothing of the Devil Man save that he is the greatest witch-doctor in the world, and on nights when the moon is up and certain stars are in their places he comes like a ghost, and we are all afraid. Then those of us who need him go forth into the forest, and he gives to us according to our desires."

"How carried he the drug?"

"Lord, it was in a crystal rod, such as white men carry their medicines in. I will bring it to you."

He went back to his hut and returned a few minutes later with a phial, the fellow to that which was already in Sanders' possession. The Commissioner took it and smelt at the opening. There was the faintest odour of almonds, and Sanders whistled, for he recognised the after-scent of cyanide of potassium, which is not such a drug as untutored witch-doctors know, much less employ.

"I can only suggest," wrote Sanders to headquarters, "that by some mischance the medicine chest of the late Sir George Carsley has come into the possession of a native 'doctor.' You will remember that the chest was with the professor when he was drowned. It has possibly been washed up and discovered.... In the meantime, I am making diligent inquiries as to the identity of the Devil Man, who seems to have leapt into fame so suddenly."

There were sleepless nights ahead for Sanders, nights of swift marchings and doublings, of quick runs up the river, of unexpected arrivals in villages, of lonely vigils in the forest and by strange pools. But he had no word of the Devil Man, though he learnt many things of interest. Most potent of his magical possessions was a box, "so small," said one who had seen it, and indicated a six-inch square. In this box dwelt a small and malicious god who pinched and scratched (yet without leaving a mark), who could stick needles into the human body and never draw blood.

"I give it up," said Sanders in despair, and went back to his base to think matters out.

He was sitting at dinner one night, when far away on the river the drum beat. It was not the regular *lo-koli* roll, but a series of staccato tappings, and, stepping softly to the door, the Commissioner listened.

He had borrowed the Houssa signalling staff from headquarters, and stationed them at intervals along the river. On a still night the tapping of a drum carries far, but the rattle of iron-wood sticks on a hollowed tree-trunk carries farthest of all.

"Clok-clok, clockitty-clock."

It sounded like the far-away croaking of a bull-frog; but Sanders picked out the letters:

"Devil Man sacrifices to-morrow night in the Forest of Dreams."

As he jotted down the message on the white sleeve of his jacket, Abiboo came running up the path.

"I have heard," said Sanders briefly. "There is steam in the *pucapuc*?"

"We are ready, master," said the man.

Sanders waited only to take a hanging revolver from the wall and throw his overcoat over his arm, for his travelling kit was already deposited on the *Zaire*, and had been for three days.

In the darkness the sharp nose of his little boat swung out to the stream, and ten minutes after the message came the boat was threshing a way against the swift river.

All night long the steamer went on, tacking from bank to bank to avoid the shoals.

Dawn found her at a wooding, where her men, working at fever speed, piled logs on her deck until she had the appearance of a timber-boat.

Then off again, stopping only to secure news of the coming sacrifice from the spies who were scattered up and down the river.

Sanders reached the edge of the Dream Forest at midnight and tied up. He had ten Houssa policemen with him, and at the head of these he stepped ashore into the blackness of the forest. One of the soldiers went ahead to find the path and keep it, and in single file the little force began its two-hour march. Once they came upon two leopards fighting; once they stumbled over a buffalo sleeping in their path. Twice they disturbed strange beasts that slunk into the shadows as they passed, and came snuffling after them, till Sanders flashed a white beam from his electric lamp in their direction. Eventually they came stealthily to the place of sacrifice.

There were at least six hundred people squatting in a semi-circle before a rough altar built of logs. Two huge fires blazed and crackled on either side of the altar; but Sanders' eyes were for the Devil Man, who leant over the body of a young girl, apparently asleep, stretched upon the logs.

Once the Devil Man had worn the garb of civilisation; now he was clothed in rags. He stood in his grimy shirt-sleeves, his white beard wild and uncombed, his pale face tense, and a curious light in his eyes. In his hand was a bright scalpel, and he was speaking—and, curiously enough, in English.

"This, gentlemen," said he, leaning easily against the rude altar, and speaking with the assurance of one who had delivered many such lectures, "is a bad case of trynosomiasis. You will observe the discoloration of skin, the opalescent pupils, and now that I have placed the patient under anaesthetics you will remark the misplacement of the cervical glands, which is an invariable symptom."

He paused and looked benignly around.

"I may say that I have lived for a great time amongst native people. I occupied the honourable position of witch-doctor in Central Africa——"

He stopped and passed his hand across his brow, striving to recall something; then he picked up the thread of his discourse.

All the time he spoke the half-naked assembly sat silent and awe-stricken, comprehending nothing save that the witch-doctor with the white face, who had come from nowhere and had done many wonderful things—his magic box proved to be a galvanic battery—was about to perform strange rites.

"Gentlemen," the old man went on, tapping the breast of his victim with the handle of his scalpel, "I shall make an incision——"

Sanders came from his place of concealment, and walked steadily towards the extemporised operating-table.

"Professor," he said gently, and the madman looked at him with a puzzled frown.

"You are interrupting the clinic," he said testily; "I am demonstrating——"

"I know, sir."

Sanders took his arm, and Sir George Carsley, a great scientist, consulting surgeon to St. Mark's Hospital, London, and the author of many books on tropical diseases, went with him like a child.

CHAPTER XII.
THE LONELY ONE.

Mr. Commissioner Sanders had lived so long with native people that he had absorbed not a little of their simplicity. More than this, he had acquired the uncanny power of knowing things which he would not and could not have known unless he were gifted with the prescience which is every aboriginal's birthright.

He had sent three spies into the Isisi country—which lies a long way from headquarters and is difficult of access—and after two months of waiting they came to him in a body, bearing good news.

This irritated Sanders to an unjustifiable degree.

"Master, I say to you that the Isisi are quiet," protested one of the spies; "and there is no talk of war."

"H'm!" said Sanders, ungraciously. "And you?"

He addressed the second spy.

"Lord," said the man, "I went into the forest, to the border of the land, and there is no talk of war. Chiefs and headmen told me this."

"Truly you are a great spy," scoffed Sanders; "and how came you to the chiefs and headmen? And how did they greet you? 'Hail! secret spy of Sandi'? Huh!"

He dismissed the men with a wave of his hand, and putting on his helmet went down to the Houssa lines, where the blue-coated soldiers gambled in the shade of their neat white barracks.

The Houssa captain was making palatable medicine with the aid of a book of cigarette papers and a six-ounce bottle of quinine sulphide.

Sanders observed his shaking hand, and talked irritably.

"There's trouble in the Isisi," he said, "I can smell it. I don't know what it is—but there's devilry of sorts."

"Secret societies?" suggested the Houssa.

"Secret grandmothers," snarled Sanders. "How many men have you got?"

"Sixty, including the lame 'uns," said the Houssa officer, and swallowed a paperful of quinine with a grimace.

Sanders tapped the toe of his boot with his thin ebony stick, and was thoughtful.

"I may want 'em," he said. "I'm going to find out what's wrong with these Isisi people."

By the little river that turns abruptly from the River of Spirits, Imgani, the Lonely One, built a house. He built it in proper fashion, stealing the wood from a village five miles away. In this village there had been many deaths, owing to The Sickness; and it is the custom on the Upper River that whenever a person dies, the house wherein he died shall die also.

No man takes shelter under the accursed roof whereunder the Spirit sits brooding; the arms of the dead man are broken and scattered on his shallow grave, and the cooking-pots of his wives are there likewise.

By and by, under the combined influences of wind and rain, the reed roof sags and sinks, the doorposts rot; elephant-grass, coarse and strong, shoots up between crevices in wall and roof; then come a heavier rain and a heavier wind, and the forest has wiped the foul spot clean.

Imgani, who said he was of the N'Gombi people, and was afraid of no devils—at any rate, no Isisi devil—stole doorposts and native rope fearlessly. He stole them by night, when the moon was behind the trees, and mocked the dead spirits, calling them by evil and tantalising names.

Yet he went cautiously to work; for whilst he did not hold spirits in account, he was wholesomely respectful of the live Isisi, who would have put him to death had his sacrilege been detected, though, strangely enough, death was the thing he feared least.

So he stole the accursed supports and accursed roof-props, and would have stolen the roofs as well, but for the fact that they were very old and full of spiders.

All these things he came and took, carrying them five miles to the turn of the river, and there, at his leisure, he built a little house. In the daytime he slept, in the night he trapped beasts and caught fish, but he made no attempt to catch the big bats that come over from the middle island of the river, though these are very edible, and regarded as a delicacy.

One day, just before the sun went down, he went into the forest on the track of zebra. He carried two big hunting-spears, such as the N'Gombi make best; a wickerwork shield, and on his back, slung by a strip of hide, a bunch of dried fish he had caught in the river.

A man of middle height was Imgani, spare of build, but broad of shoulder. His skin shone healthily, and his step was light. As he walked, you saw the muscles of his back ripple and weave like the muscles of a well-trained thoroughbred.

He was half an hour's journey within the forest, when he came upon a girl. She was carrying a bundle of manioc root on her head, and walked gracefully.

When she saw Imgani she stopped dead, and the fear of death and worse came in her eyes, for she knew him to be an outcast man, with no tribe and no people. Such men are more dreadful than the ingali, who rears up from the grass and plunges his poison-fangs in your leg.

They stood watching one another, the man leaning with both hands on the spears, his cheek against them; the girl trembled.

"Woman, where do you go?" said Imgani.

"Master, I go to the village which is by the river, this being the path," she flurried.

"What have you there?"

"Manioc, for bread," she whispered thickly.

"You are a root-eater," said Imgani, nodding his head.

"Master, let me go," she said, staring at him.

Imgani jerked his head.

"I see you are afraid of me—yet I want nothing from you," he said. "I am Imgani, which means the Lonely One; and I have no desire for wives or women, being too high a man for such folly. You are safe, root-eater, for if I wished I would fill this forest with the daughters of chiefs, all very beautiful, all moaning for me."

The girl's fear had disappeared, and she looked at him curiously. Moreover, she recognised that there was truth in his claim of austerity. Possibly she was a little piqued, for she said tartly enough, employing an Isisi proverb:

"Only the goat bleats at the mouth of the leopard's cave—the Isisi grow fat on strangers."

He looked at her, his head cocked on one side.

"They say in the lower country that the Isisi sell men to the Arabi," he said musingly. "That is bad talk; you may go."

With another jerk of his head he dismissed her.

She had gone some little distance when he called her back.

"Root-eater," he said, "if men ask you who I be, you shall say that I am Imgani the Lonely One, who is a prince amongst the princes; also that I have killed many men in my day—so many that I cannot count them. Also say that from my house, which I have built by the river, to as far as a man can see in every way, is my kingdom, and let none stray therein, except to bring gifts in their hands, for I am very terrible and very jealous."

"Lord," said the girl, "I will say all this."

And she went, half running, in the direction of the village, leaving Imgani to continue on his way.

Now this village had many young men eager to please the girl, who carried manioc, for she was a chief's daughter, and she was, moreover, fourteen, a marriageable age. So when she came flying along the village street, half hysterical in her fear, crying, babbling, incoherent, there was not wanting sympathy nor knight valiant to wipe out the insult.

Six young men, with spears and short swords, danced before the chief and the chief's daughter (how important she felt, any woman of any race will tell you), and one of them, E'kebi, a man gifted with language, described from sunset to moonrise, which is roughly four hours, exactly what would happen to Imgani when the men of the Isisi fell upon him; how his eyes would shrivel as before a great and terrible fire, and his limbs wither up, and divers other physiological changes which need not be particularised.

"That is good talk," said the chief; "yet, since Sandi is our master and has spies everywhere, do not shed blood, for the smell of blood is carried farther than a man can see. And Sandi is very devilish on this question of killing. Moreover, this Lonely One is a stranger, and if we catch him we may sell him to the Arabi, who will give us cloth and gin for him."

Having heard all this, they sacrificed a young goat and marched. They came upon the house of Imgani, but the Lonely One was not there, for he was trapping beasts in the forest; so they burnt his house, uprooted his poor garden, and, being joined by many other Isisi people, who had followed at a respectful distance, lest Imgani's estimate of his own prowess were justified by results, they held high revel, until of a sudden the sun came up over the middle island, and all the little stars in the sky went out.

Imgani saw all this, leaning on his spears in the shadow of the forest, but was content to be a spectator.

For, he reasoned, if he went out against them they would attempt to kill him or beat him with rods, and that his high spirit could not endure.

He saw the flames lick away the house he had built with such labour.

"They are foolish people," he mused, "for they burn their own, and perhaps the spirits of the dead will be displeased and give them boils."

When all that was left of his habitation was a white heap of ash, a dark-red glow, and a hazy wisp of smoke, Imgani turned his face to the forest.

All day long he walked, halting only to eat the fish he carried, and at night time he came upon another Isisi village, which was called O'Fasi.

He came through the village street with his shoulders squared, his head erect, swinging his spears famously. He looked neither to the left nor to the right; and the villagers, crowding to the doors of their huts, put their clenched knuckles to their mouths, and said: "O ho!" which means that they were impressed.

So he stalked through the entire length of the village, and was making for the forest-path beyond, when a messenger came pattering after him.

"Lord," said the messenger, "the *capita* of this village, who is responsible to the Government for all people who pass, and especially for thieves who may have escaped from the Village of Irons, desires your presence, being sure that you are no thief, but a great one, and wishing to do honour to you."

Thus he recited, and being a peaceable man, who had been chosen for the part because he was related by marriage to the principal wife of the chief, he kept a cautious eye on the broad-headed spear, and determined the line of his flight.

"Go back to your master, slave," said Imgani, "and say to him that I go to find a spot of sufficient loneliness, where I may sleep this night and occupy myself with high thoughts. When I have found such a place I will return. Say, also, that I am a prince of my own people, and that my father has legions of such quantity that, if every fighting man of the legions were to take a handful of sand from the bottom of the river, the river would be bottomless; also say that I am named Imgani, and that I love myself better than any man has loved himself since the moon went white that it might not look like the sun."

He went on, leaving the messenger filled with thought.

True to his promise, Imgani returned.

He came back to find that there was a palaver in progress, the subject of the palaver being the unfortunate relative by marriage to the chief's principal wife.

"Who," the chief was saying, "has put shame upon me, being as great a fool as his cousin, my wife."

"Master," said the poor relation humbly, "I entreated him to return; but he was a man of great pride, and, moreover, impatient to go."

"Your mother was a fool," said the chief; "her mother also was a fool, and your father, whoever he was, and no man knows, was a great fool."

This interesting beginning to a crude address on hereditary folly was interrupted by the return of Imgani, and as he came slowly up the little hillock the assembly took stock of him, from the square, steel razor stuck in the tight-fitting leopard-skin cap to the thin bangles of brass about his ankles.

The chief, a portly man of no great courage, observed the spears, noting that the hafts were polished smooth by much handling.

"Lord," said he mildly, "I am chief of this village, appointed by the Government, who gave me a medal to wear about my neck, bearing on one side the picture of a great man with a beard, and on the other side certain devil marks and writings of vast power. This was given to me that all people might know I was chief, but I have lost the medal. None the less, I am chief of this village, as this will show."

He fumbled in the bosom of his cloth and brought out a bag of snake skin, and from this he extracted a very soiled paper.

With tender care he unfolded it, and disclosed a sheet of official notepaper with a few scrawled words in the handwriting of Mr. Commissioner Sanders. They ran:

"To all Sub-Commissioners, Police Officers, and Commanders of Houssa Ports:

"Arrest and detain the bearer if found in any other territory than the Isisi."

There was a history attached to this singular document. It had to do with an unauthorised raid upon certain Ochori villages and a subsequent trial at headquarters, where a chief, all aquiver with apprehension, listened to a terse but knowledgable prophecy as to what fate awaited him if he put foot out of his restricted dominion.

Imgani took the paper in his hand and was interested. He turned it about, rubbed the writing lightly with his fingers to see whether it was permanent, and returned it to the chief.

"That is very wonderful, though I do not fear magic, except an especial kind such as is practised by a certain witch-doctor of my father's," he said; "nor do I know any government which can govern me."

After which he proceeded to tell them of his father, and of his legions and wives, and various other matters of equal interest.

"I do not doubt that you will understand me," he said. "I am a Lonely One, hating the company of men, who are as changeable as the snow upon the mountains. Therefore, I have left my house with my wives, who were faithful as women go, and I have taken with me no legion, since they are my father's."

The chief was puzzled.

"Why you are lonely, I cannot tell," he said; "but certainly you did right to leave your father's legions. This is a great matter, which needs a palaver of older men."

And he ordered the *lo-koli* to be sounded and the elders of the village to be assembled.

They came, bringing their own carved stools, and sat about the thatched shelter, where the chief sat in his presidency.

Again Imgani told his story; it was about fifty wives, and legions of warriors as countless as the sand of the river's beach; and the trustful Isisi listened and believed.

"And I need this," said Imgani, in his peroration; "a little house built on the edge of the river, in such a place that no path passes me and no human being comes within sight of me, for I am very lonely by nature—and a great hater of men."

Imgani went to live in the clearing Nature had made for him, and in a hut erected by his new-found friends. Other hospitalities he refused.

"I have no wish for wives," he stated, "being full of mighty plans to recover my kingdom from evil men who are my father's councillors."

Lonely he was in very truth, for none saw him except on very special occasions. It was his practice to go hunting by night and to sleep away the hot days. Sometimes, when the red ball of the sun dropped down behind the trees on the western bank of the river, the villagers saw the straight, blue film of his smoke as he cooked his evening meal; sometimes a homeward-bound boatman saw him slipping silently through the thin edge of the forest on his way to a kill.

They called him the Silent One, and he enjoyed a little fame.

More than this, he enjoyed the confidence of his hosts. The Isisi country is within reach of the Foreign River, down which strangely-shaped boats come by night empty, and return by night full of people who are chained neck to neck, and the officials of French West Africa—which adjoins the Isisi country—receive stories of raids and of burnings which they have not the facilities for investigating, for the Isisi border is nearly six hundred miles from the French headquarters, and lies through a wilderness.

Imgani, in his hunting trips, saw things which might have filled him with amazement, but for the fact that he was a man who was not given to emotion.

He saw little caravans that came stealing from the direction of the territory of France, with whimpering women and groaning men in bondage.

He saw curious midnight shippings of human souls, and grew to know the white-robed Arabs who handled the whip so deftly.

One night as he stood watching all these things, El Mahmud, that famous trader, espied him in the moonlight and saw that he was of a strange people.

"What man are you?" he asked.

"Lord," said Imgani, "I am of a strange people—the N'Gombi."

"That is a lie," said the slaver, "for you have not the face marks of the N'Gombi; you are a half-bred Arab," and he addressed him in Arabic.

Imgani shook his head.

"He does not understand," said the slaver to his lieutenant; "find out where this man's hut is; one night we will take him, for he is worth money."

He spoke in Arabic, and his subordinate nodded.

When the slaver came again three men visited Imgani's house, but he was hunting, and he was hunting every time the long boats came by night to O'Fasi.

Sanders did not go to O'Fasi for six months, during which time, it should be emphasised, nothing happened which by any stretch of imagination could be held to justify any loss of prestige.

He was due to make his half-yearly visit to the Isisi. The crops had been good, the fish plentiful, the rains gentle, and there had been no sickness. All these facts you may bear in mind.

One morning, when swirls of grey mist looped from tree to tree and the east was growing grey, Imgani came back from the forest bearing on his shoulders all that was material of a small buck which he had snared in the night.

When he saw a little fire before his hut and a man squatting chin on knee, he twirled those spears of his cheerfully and went on, for he was afraid of no man.

"Is the world so full of people that you come to disturb my loneliness?" he asked. "I have a thought that I shall kill you and fry your heart, for I do not like to see you sitting by a fire before my hut."

He said all this with a ferocious mien, and the man before the fire shifted uneasily.

"Master, I expected this," he said, "for I see you are a proud man; but I come because of your pride, knowing your wisdom."

Imgani tossed the buck to one side and sat down, staring threateningly and laying the haft of his spears across his bare knee.

Then the other man craned his neck forward and spoke eagerly.

The sun came up and flushed the world rosy; but still he sat talking with great force, Imgani listening.

"So, master," he concluded, "we will kill Sandi when he comes to palaver. Ifiba, M'bwka, and a cousin of my mother's, will put spears into him very quickly, and we shall be a great people."

Imgani nodded his head wisely.

"That is true," he said, "people who kill white men must be greatly honoured, because all the other nations will say: 'Behold, these are the people who kill white men!'"

"And when he is dead," the messenger went on, "many young men will go to the boat that smokes and slay all who are with him."

"That is wise also," said Imgani; "when I kill white men I also kill their friends."

He discussed his deeds to some length and with great detail. After the man had gone, Imgani made a meal of fish and manioc, polished the steel blades of his spears with wet sand, dried them carefully with grass, and laid himself down in the shade of the hut to sleep.

He was awake in the early part of the afternoon, and went plunging into the river, swimming far towards the middle stream with great, strong strokes.

Then he swam back to shore, let the sun dry him, and dressed himself in his leopard skin.

He came to the village slowly, and found it agitated. More especially so was the chief, that wise *capita*, for news had arrived that Sandi was coming in the night, and that even now his steamer was rounding the bend of the river.

A plan had miscarried; Sanders was two days ahead of time, and Ifiba and M'bwka, his trusty men, were away on an expedition, and there was no time to substitute unseasoned assassins.

The steamer drifted broadside to the shore, one stern wheel revolving lazily, and then they saw, Imgani amongst the rest, that the decks were crowded with soldiers, impassive brown men in blue uniforms and fezes.

A plank bumped down, and holding their rifles high the soldiers came pattering to the shore, and with them a white officer but not Sandi.

It was a brusque, white man.

"Who is the chief here?" he said crossly.

"Lord, I am that man," said the stout chief, all a-flutter.

"Take that man."

A sergeant of Houssas grasped the chief and deftly swung him round; a corporal of Houssas snapped a pair of handcuffs on his wrists.

"Lord," he whined, "why this shame?"

"Because you are a great thief," said the Houssa officer, "a provoker of war and a dealer in slaves."

"If any man says that, it is a lie," said the chief, "for no Government man has witnessed such abominations."

Imgani stepped forward.

"Chief," he said, "I have seen it."

"You are a great liar," fumed the portly *capita*, trembling with rage, "and Sandi, who is my friend, will not believe you."

"I am Sandi," said Imgani, and smiled crookedly.

CHAPTER XIII.
THE SEER.

There are many things that happen in the very heart of Africa that no man can explain; that is why those who know Africa best hesitate to write stories about it.

Because a story about Africa must be a mystery story, and your reader of fiction requires that his mystery shall be, in the end, X-rayed so that the bones of it are visible.

You can no more explain many happenings which are the merest commonplaces in latitude 2° N., longitude (say) 46° W., than you can explain the miracle of faith, or the wonder of telepathy, as this story goes to show.

In the dead of a night Mr. Commissioner Sanders woke.

His little steamer was tied up by a wooding—a wooding he had prepared for himself years before by lopping down trees and leaving them to rot.

He was one day's steam either up or down the river from the nearest village, but he was only six hours' march from the Amatombo folk, who live in the very heart of the forest, and employ arrows poisoned by tetanus.

Sanders sat up in bed and listened.

A night bird chirped monotonously; he heard the "clug-clug" of water under the steamer's bows and the soft rustling of leaves as a gentle breeze swayed the young boughs of the trees that overhung the boat. Very intently he listened, then reached down for his mosquito boots and his socks.

He drew them on, found his flannel coat hanging behind the door of his tiny cabin, and opened the door softly. Then he waited, standing, his head bent.

In the darkness he grinned unpleasantly, and, thumbing back the leather strap that secured the flap of the holster which hung by his bunk he slipped out the Colt-automatic, and noiselessly pulled back the steel envelope.

He was a careful man, not easily flurried, and his every movement was methodical. He was cautious enough to push up the little safety-catch which prevents premature explosion, tidy enough to polish the black barrel on the soft sleeve of his coat, and he waited a long time before he stepped out into the hot darkness of the night.

By and by he heard again the sound which had aroused him. It was the faint twitter of a weaver bird.

Now weaver birds go to sleep at nights like sensible people, and they live near villages, liking the society of human beings. Certainly they do not advertise their presence so brazenly as did this bird, who twittered and twittered at intervals.

Sanders watched patiently.

Then suddenly, from close at hand, from the very deck on which he stood, came an answering call.

Sanders had his little cabin on the bridge of the steamer; he walked farther away from it. In the corner of the bridge he crouched down, his thumb on the safety-catch.

He felt, rather than saw, a man come from the forest; he knew that there was one on board the steamer who met him.

Then creeping round the deck-house came two men. He could just discern the bulk of them as they moved forward till they found the door of the cabin and crept in. He heard a little noise, and grinned again, though he knew that their spear-heads were making sad havoc of his bedclothes.

Then there was a little pause, and he saw one come out by himself and look around.

He turned to speak softly to the man inside.

Sanders rose noiselessly.

The man in the doorway said "Kah!" in a gurgling voice and went down limply, because Sanders had kicked him scientifically in the stomach, which is a native's weak spot. The second man ran out, but fell with a crash over the Commissioner's extended leg, and, falling, received the full weight of a heavy pistol barrel in the neighbourhood of his right ear.

"Yoka!" called Sanders sharply, and there was a patter of feet aft, for your native is a light sleeper, "tie these men up. Get steam, for we will go away from here; it is not a nice place."

Sanders, as I have tried to explain, was a man who knew the native; he thought like a native, and there were moments when he acted not unlike a barbarian.

Clear of the danger, he tied up to a little island in mid-stream just as the dawn spread greyly, and hustled his two prisoners ashore.

"My men," said he, "you came to kill me in the dark hours."

"Lord, that is true," said one, "I came to kill, and this other man, who is my brother, told me when to come—yet it might have been another whom he called, for I am but one of many."

Sanders accepted the fact that a chain of cheerful assassins awaited his advent without any visible demonstration of annoyance.

"Now you will tell me," he said, "who gave the word for the killing, and why I must die."

The man he addressed, a tall, straight youth of the Amatombo people, wiped the sweat from his forehead with his manacled hands.

"Lord, though you chop me," he said, "I will not tell you, for I have a great ju-ju, and there are certain fetishes which would be displeased."

Sanders tried the other man with no greater success. This other was a labourer he had taken on at a village four days' journey down stream.

"Lord, if I die for my silence I will say nothing," he said.

"Very good," said Sanders, and nodded his head to Abiboo. "I shall stake you out," he added, "flat on the ground, your legs and arms outstretched, and I will light a little fire on your chests, and by and by you will tell me all I want to know."

Staked out they were, with fluffy little balls of dried creeper on each breast, and Sanders took a lighted stick from the fire his servants had built.

The men on the ground watched his every movement. They saw him blow the red stick to a flame and advance toward them, then one said—

"Lord, I will speak."

"So I thought," said Sanders; "and speak truth, or I will make you uncomfortable."

If you ask me whether Sanders would have employed his lighted stick, I answer truthfully that I think it possible; perhaps Sanders knew his men better than I know Sanders.

The two men, released from their unhappy position, talked frankly, and Sanders was a busy man taking notes in English of the conversation which was mainly in Bomongo.

When his interrogation was completed, Sanders gathered up his notes and had the men taken on board the steamer. Two hours later the *Zaire* was moving at its fullest speed in the direction of a village of the Akasava, which is called in the native tongue Tukalala.

There was a missionary to Tukalala, a devoted young American Methodist, who had elected to live in the fever belt amongst heathen men that he might bring their hearts to the knowledge of God.

Sanders had no special regard for missionaries; indeed, he had views on the brotherhood which did him no particular credit, but he had an affection for the young man who laboured so cheerfully with such unpromising material, and now he paced the little bridge of his steamer impatiently, for it was very necessary that he should reach Tukalala before certain things happened.

He came round a bend of the little river just as the sun was going down behind the trees on the western bank, and the white beach before the mission station showed clearly.

He motioned with two fingers to the man at the wheel, and the little steamer swung almost broadside to the swift stream and headed for the bank, and the black water of the river humped up against his port bow as though it were a sluice gate.

Into the beach he steamed; "pucka-pucka-pucka-puck," sang the stern wheel noisily.

Where the missionary's house had stood was a chaos of blackened debris, and out of it rose lazy little wisps of smoke.

He found the missionary dressed in white duck, greatly soiled, lying face downwards, and he found some difficulty in raising him, because he was pinned to the ground with a broad-bladed elephant spear which had been broken off flush with his shoulders.

Sanders turned him on his back, closed the patient's eyes, staring, it seemed, hungrily at the darkening sky as though at the last questioning God's wisdom.

The Commissioner took a gaudy bandana handkerchief from his pocket, and laid it on the dead man's face.

"Abiboo," he said softly to his sergeant, "dig me a great hole by that copal gum, for this man was a great chief amongst his people, and had communion with gods."

"He was a Christ man," said Abiboo sagely, who was a devout follower of the Prophet, "and in the Sura of Mary it is written:

"'The sects have fallen to variance about Jesus, but woe, because of the assembly of a great day to those who believe not!'"

Abiboo bore the title of Haj because he had been to Mecca and knew the Koran better than most Christians know the Bible.

Sanders said nothing. He took a cigar from his pocket and lit it, casting his eyes around.

No building stood. Where the mission station with its trim garden had been, was desolation. He saw scraps of cloth in the fading light. These were other victims, he knew.

In the mellow light of the moon he buried the missionary, saying the Lord's Prayer over him, and reciting as much of the Burial Service as he could remember.

Then he went back to the *Zaire* and set a guard. In the morning Sanders turned the nose of the *Zaire* down stream, and at sunset came to the big river—he had been sailing a tributary—and where the two rivers meet is the city of the Akasava.

They brought the paramount chief of all the people to him, and there was a palaver on the little bridge with a lantern placed on the deck and one limp candle therein to give light to the assembly.

"Chief," said Sanders, "there is a dead white man in your territory, and I will have the hearts of the men who killed him, or by The Death I will have your head."

He said this evenly, without passion, yet he swore by *Ewa*, which means death and is a most tremendous oath. The chief, squatting on the deck, fidgeting with his hands, shivered.

"Lord," he said, in a cracked voice, "this is a business of which I know nothing; this thing has happened in my territory, but so far from my hand that I can neither punish nor reward."

Sanders was silent save for an unsympathetic sniff.

"Also, master," said the chief, "if the truth be told, this palaver is not of the Akasava alone, for all along the big river men are rebellious, obeying a new ju-ju more mighty than any other."

"I know little of ju-jus," said Sanders shortly, "only I know that a white man has died and his spirit walks abroad and will not rest until I have slain men. Whether it be you or another I do not care—the palaver is finished."

The chief rose awkwardly, brought up his hand in salute, and went shuffling down the sloping plank to land.

As for Sanders, he sat thinking, smoking one cigar after another. He sat long into the night. Once he called his servant to replace the candle in the lantern and bring him a cushion for his head. He sat there until the buzzing little village hushed to sleep, until there was no sound but the whispering of bat wings as they came and went from the middle island—for bats love islands, especially the big vampire bats.

At two o'clock in the morning he looked at his watch, picked up the lantern, and walked aft.

He picked a way over sleeping men until he came to that part of the deck where a Houssa squatted with loaded carbine watching the two prisoners.

He stirred them gently with his foot, and they sat up blinking at his light.

"You must tell me some more," he said. "How came this bad ju-ju to your land?"

The man he addressed looked up at him.

"Lord, how comes rain or wind?" he said. "It was a sudden thought amongst the people. There were certain rites and certain dances, and we chopped a man; then we all painted our faces with camwood, and the maidens said 'Kill!'"

Sanders could be very patient.

"I am as your father and your mother," he said. "I carry you in my arms; when the waters came up and destroyed your gardens I came with manioc and salt and saved you; when the sickness came I brought white men who scraped your arms and put magic in your blood; I have made peace, and your wives are safe from M'Gombi and Isisi folk, yet you are for killing me."

The other nodded.

"That is true talk, master—but such is the way of ju-jus. They are very High Things, and do not remember."

141

Sanders was worried; this matter was out of his reach. "What said the ju-ju?"

"Lord, it said very clearly, speaking through the mouth of an old man, M'fabaka of Begeli——"

"M'fabaka of Begeli?" repeated Sanders softly, and noted the name for a speedy hanging.

"This old man saw a vision, and in this vision, which he saw with great pain and foaming at the mouth and hot eyeballs, he saw white men slain by black men and their houses burnt."

"When was this?"

"When the moon was full"—six days ago, thought Sanders—"and he saw a great king with many legions marching through the land making all white men fear him."

He went on to give, as only a native memory can recall, the minutest detail of the king's march; how he slew white men and women and put their house to flames; how his legions went dancing before him.

"And all this happened at the full of the moon," he finished; "therefore we, too, went out to slay, and, knowing that your Highness would be coming as is your custom to give judgment at this season of the year, it was thought wise to kill you, also the Christ-man."

He told all this in a matter-of-fact tone, and Sanders knew that he spoke the truth.

Another man would have been more affected by that portion of the narrative which touched him most nearly, but it was the king ("a great man, very large about the middle"), and his devastating legions who occupied the Commissioner's thoughts.

There was truth behind this, he did not doubt that. There was a rising somewhere that he had not heard of; very quickly he passed in mental review the kings of the adjoining territories and of his own lands.

Bosambo of Monrovia, that usurper of the Ochori chieftainship, sent him from time to time news of the outlying peoples. There was no war, north or south or east.

"I will see this old man M'fabaka of Begeli," he said.

Begeli is a village that lies on an in-running arm of the river, so narrow that it seems like a little river, so still that it is apparently a lake. Forests of huge trees slope down on either bank, and the trees are laced one to the other with great snake-like tendrils, and skirted at foot with rank undergrowth. The *Zaire* came cautiously down this stretch of calm water, two Maxim guns significantly displayed at the bridge.

A tiny little steamer this *Zaire*. She had the big blue of England drooping from the flagstaff high above the stern wheel—an ominous sign, for when Sanders flew the Commissioner's flag it meant trouble for somebody.

He stood on the deck coatless, signalling with his raised fingers to the man at the wheel.

"Phew!" An arrow was shivering in the wooden deck-house. He pulled it out and examined its hammered steel point carefully, then he threw it overboard.

"Bang!"

A puff of smoke from the veiling foliage—a bullet splintered the back of his deck-chair.

He reached down and took up a rifle, noticed the drift of the smoke and took careful aim.

"Bang!"

There was no sign to show where the bullet struck, and the only sound that came back was the echo and the shrill swish of it as it lashed its way through the green bushes.

There was no more shooting.

"Puck-apuck-puck-apuck-puck," went the stern wheel slowly, and the bows of the *Zaire* clove the calm waters and left a fan of foam behind. Before the village was in view six war canoes, paddling abreast, came out to meet the Commissioner. He rang the engines to "Stop," and as the noise of them died away he could hear in the still air the beating of drums; through his glasses he saw fantastically-painted bodies, also a head stuck upon a spear.

There had been a trader named Ogilvie in this part of the world, a mild, uncleanly man who sold cloth and bought wild rubber.

"Five hundred yards," said Sanders, and Sergeant Abiboo, fiddling with the grip of the port Maxim, gave the cartridge belt a little pull, swung the muzzle forward, and looked earnestly along the sights. At the same time the Houssa corporal, who stood by the tripod of the starboard gun, sat down on the little saddle seat of it with his thumb on the control.

There came a spurt of smoke from the middle canoe; the bullet fell short.

"Ogilvie, my man," soliloquised Sanders, "if you are alive—which I am sure you are not—you will explain to me the presence of these Schneiders."

Nearer came the canoes, the paddle plunging rhythmically, a low, fierce drone of song accompanying the movement.

"Four hundred yards," said Sanders, and the men at the Maxims readjusted the sights.

"The two middle canoes," said Sanders. "Fire!"

A second pause.

"Ha, ha, ha, ha, ha, ha, ha, ha!" laughed the guns sardonically.

Sanders watched the havoc through his glasses.

"The other canoes," he said briefly.

"Ha, ha, ha, ha, ha, ha, ha, ha!"

This gunner was a careful man, and fired spasmodically, desiring to see the effects of his shots.

Sanders saw men fall, saw one canoe sway and overturn, and the black heads of men in the water; he rang the steamer ahead full speed.

Somebody fired a shot from one of the uninjured canoes. The wind of the bullet fanned his face, he heard the smack of it as it struck the woodwork behind.

There came another shot, and the boy at the wheel turned his head with a little grin to Sanders.

"Lord," he mumbled in Arabic, "this was ordained from the beginning."

Sanders slipped his arm about his shoulder and lowered him gently to the deck.

"All things are with God," he said softly.

"Blessed be His name," whispered the dying boy.

Sanders caught the wheel as it spun and beckoned another steersman forward.

The nose of the steamer had turned to the offending canoe. This was an unhappy circumstance for the men therein, for both guns now covered it, and they rattled together, and through the blue haze you saw the canoe emptied.

That was the end of the fight. A warrior in the fifth boat held his spear horizontally above his head in token of surrender, and ten minutes later the chief of the rebels was on board.

"Master," he said calmly, as they led him to Sanders' presence, "this is a bad palaver. How will you deal with me?"

Sanders looked at him steadily.

"I will be merciful with you," he said, "for as soon as we come to the village I shall hang you."

"So I thought," said the chief without moving a muscle; "and I have heard it said that you hang men very quickly so that they feel little pain."

"That is my practice," said Sanders of the River, and the chief nodded his head approvingly.

"I would rather it were so," he said.

It was to a sorrowful village that he came, for there were many women to wail their dead.

Sanders landed with his Houssas and held a high palaver under the trees.

"Bring me the old man M'fabaka who sees visions," he said, and they brought him a man so old that he had nothing but bones to shape him.

They carried him to the place of justice and set him down before the Commissioner.

"You are an evil man," said Sanders, "and because your tongue has lied many men have died; to-day I hang your chief upon a tree, and with him certain others. If you stand before your people and say, 'Such a story, and such a story was a lie and no other thing,' you may live your days; but, if you persist in your lying, by my God, and your god, you shall die!"

It was a long time before the old man spoke, for he was very old and very frightened, and the fear of death, which is the ghost of some old men, was on him.

"I spoke the truth," he quavered at last. "I spoke of what I saw and of what I knew—only that." Sanders waited.

"I saw the great king slay and burn; yesterday I saw him march his regiments to war, and there was a great shouting, and I saw smoke."

He shook his head helplessly.

"I saw these things. How can I say I saw nothing?"

"What manner of king?" asked Sanders.

Again there was a long interval of silence whilst the old man collected himself.

"A great king," he said shakily, "as big as a bull about the middle, and he wore great, white feathers and the skin of a leopard."

"You are mad," said Sanders, and ended the palaver.

Six days later Sanders went back to headquarters, leaving behind him a chastened people.

Ill-news travels faster than steam can push a boat, and the little *Zaire*, keeping to mid-stream with the blue flag flying, was an object of interest to many small villages, the people of which crowded down to their beaches and stood with folded arms, or with clenched knuckles at their lips to signify their perturbation, and shouted in monotonous chorus after the boat.

"Oh, Sandi—father! How many evil ones have you slain to-day? Oh, killer of devils—oh, hanger of trees!—we are full of virtues and do not fear."

"Ei-fo, Kalaba? Ei ko Sandi! Eiva fo elegi," etc.

Sanders went with the stream swiftly, for he wished to establish communication with his chief. Somewhere in the country there was a revolt—that he knew.

There was truth in all the old man had said before he died—for die he did of sheer panic and age.

Who was this king in revolt? Not the king of the Isisi, or of the M'Gombi, nor of the people in the forelands beyond the Ochori.

The *Zaire* went swinging in to the Government beach, and there was a captain of Houssas to meet him.

"Land wire working?" said Sanders as he stepped ashore.

The Houssa captain nodded.

"What's the palaver?" he asked.

"War of a kind," said Sanders; "some king or other is on the rampage."

And he told the story briefly.

The Houssa officer whistled.

"By Lord High Keeper of the Privy Purse!" he swore mildly, "that's funny!"

"You've a poisonous sense of humour!" Sanders snapped.

"Hold hard," said the Houssa, and caught his arm. "Don't you know that Lo Benguela is in rebellion? The description fits him."

Sanders stopped.

"Of course," he said, and breathed a sigh of relief.

"But," said the perplexed Houssa officer, "Matabeleland is three thousand miles away. Rebellion started a week ago. How did these beggars know?"

For answer Sanders beckoned a naked man of the Akasava people who was of his boat's crew, being a good chopper of wood.

"I'fasi," he said, "tell me, what do they do in your country to-day?" The man grinned sheepishly, and stood on one leg in his embarrassment, for it was an honour to common men that Sanders should address them by name.

"Lord, they go to hunt elephant," he said.

"How many?" said Sanders.

"Two villages," said the man, "for one village has sickness and cannot go."

"How do you know this?" said Sanders. "Is not your country four days by river and three days by land?"

The man looked uncomfortable.

"It is as you say, master—yet I know," he said.

Sanders turned to the Houssa with a smile.

"There is quite a lot to be learnt in this country," he said.

A month later Sanders received a cutting from the *Cape Times*. The part which interested him ran:

" . . . the rumour generally credited by the Matabele rebels that their adherents in the north had suffered a repulse lacks confirmation. The Commissioner of Barotseland denies the native story of a rebellious tribe, and states that as far as he knows the whole of his people have remained quiet. Other northern

Commissioners state the same. There has been no sympathetic rising, though the natives are emphatic that in a 'far-away land,' which they cannot define, such a rebellion has occurred. The idea is, of course, absurd." Sanders smiled again.

CHAPTER THE LAST.
DOGS OF WAR.

Chiefest of the restrictions placed upon the black man by his white protector is that which prevents him, when his angry passions rise, from taking his enemy by the throat and carving him with a broad, curved blade of native make. Naturally, even the best behaved of the tribes chafe under this prohibition the British have made.

You may be sure that the Akasava memory is very short, and the punishment which attended their last misdoing is speedily forgotten in the opportunity and the temptation which must inevitably come as the years progress. Thus, the Akasava, learning of certain misdoings on the part of the Ochori, found themselves in the novel possession of a genuine grievance, and prepared for war, first sending a message to "Sandi," setting forth at some length the nature of the insult the Ochori had offered them. Fortunately, Sanders was in the district, and came on the spot very quickly, holding palaver, and soothing an outraged nation as best he could. Sanders was a tactful man, and tact does not necessarily imply soft-handedness. For there was a truculent soul who sat in the council and interpolated brusque questions.

Growing bolder as the Commissioner answered suavely, he went, as a child or native will, across the border line which divides a good manner from a bad. Sanders turned on him.

"What base-born slave dog are you?" he asked; and whilst the man was carefully considering his answer, Sanders kicked him down the slope of the hill on which the palaver house stood, and harmony was once more restored.

Very soon on the heels of this palaver came a bitter complaint from the Isisi. It concerned fishing nets that had been ruthlessly destroyed by the Lulungo folk, and this was a more difficult matter for Sanders to settle. For one thing, all self-respecting people hate the Lulungo, a dour, wicked, mischievous people, without shame or salt. But the Isisi were pacified, and a messy war was averted. There were other and minor alarums—all these were in the days' work—but Sanders worried about the Lulungo, because of their general badness, and because of all his people, Isisi, Ikeli, Akasava, and Ochori, who hated the Lulungo folk with a deep-rooted hatred. In his own heart, Sanders knew that war could only be postponed, and so advised London, receiving in reply, from an agitated Under-Secretary in Whitehall, the urgent request that the postponement should cover and extend beyond the conclusion of "the present financial year—for heaven's sake!"

They had a proverb up in the Lulungo district—three days' march beyond the Akasava—and it is to this effect: "When a man hath a secret enemy and cannot find him, pull down his own hut and search among the débris." This is a cumbersome translation. There is another proverb which says, "Because of the enemy who lives in the shadow of your hut"; also another which says, "If you cannot find your enemy, kill your dearest friend." The tendency of all these proverbs is to show that the Lulungo people took a gloomy view of life, and were naturally suspicious.

Sanders had a cook of the Lulungo tribe, down at M'piti—which model city served as Mr. Commissioner's headquarters. He was a wanderer, and by way of being a cosmopolitan, having travelled as far north as Dacca, and as far south as Banana—and presumably up the Congo to Matadi. When he came to M'piti, applying for work, he was asked his name and replied in the "English" of the Coast:

"Master, dey one call me Sixpence all'time. I make 'um cook fine; you look 'um for better cook, you no find 'um—savvy."

"And what," said Sanders, in the Lulungo dialect, "what mongrel talk do you call this?"

"Master, it is English," said the abashed native.

"It is monkey talk," said Sanders, cruelly; "the talk of krooboys and half-bred sailors who have no language. What are you called by your people?"

"Lataki, master," said the cook.

"So shall you be called," said Sanders. "Further, you shall speak no language but your own, and your pay will be ten shillings a month."

Lataki made a good cook, and was a model citizen for exactly three months, at the end of which time Sanders, returning unexpectedly from a hunting trip, found Lataki asleep in his master's bed—Lataki being very drunk, and two empty gin bottles by the bedside testifying mutely to his discredit. Sanders called his police, and Lataki was thrown into the lock-up to sober down, which he did in twenty-four hours.

"I would have you understand," said Sanders to the culprit the next day, "that I cannot allow my servants to get drunk; more especially I cannot allow my drunken servants to sleep off their potations on my bed."

"Lord, I am ashamed," said Lataki cheerfully; "such things happen to a man who has seen much of the world."

"You may say the same about the whipping you are about to receive," said Sanders, and gave an order to the sergeant of police.

Lataki was no stoic and when, tied to a tree, ten strokes were laid upon his stout back by a bored Houssa, he cried out very loudly against Sanders, and against that civilisation of which Sanders was the chosen instrument.

After it was all over, and he had discovered that he was still alive, albeit sore, he confessed he had received little more than he deserved, and promised tearfully that the lesson should not be without result. Sanders, who had nothing more to say in the matter, dismissed him to his duties.

It was a week after this that the Commissioner was dining in solitude on palm-oil chop—which is a delicious kind of coast curry—and chicken. He had begun his meal when he stopped suddenly, went to his office, and brought in a microscope. Then he took a little of the "chop"—just as much as might go on the end of a pin—smeared it on a specimen glass, and focussed the instrument. What he saw interested him. He put away the microscope and sent for Lataki; and Lataki, in spotless white, came.

"Lataki," said Sanders carelessly, "knowing the ways of white men, tell me how a master might do his servant honour?"

The cook in the doorway hesitated.

"There are many ways," he said, after a pause. "He might——"

He stopped, not quite sure of his ground.

"Because you are a good servant, though possessed of faults," said Sanders, "I wish to honour you; therefore I have chosen this way; you, who have slept in my bed unbidden, shall sit at my table with me at my command."

The man hesitated, a little bewildered, then he shuffled forward and sat clumsily in the chair opposite his master.

"I will wait upon you," said Sanders, "according to the custom of your own people."

He heaped two large spoonfuls of palm-oil chop upon the plate before the man.

"Eat," he said.

But the man made no movement, sitting with his eyes upon the tablecloth.

"Eat," said Sanders again, but still Lataki sat motionless.

Then Sanders rose, and went to the open doorway of his bungalow and blew a whistle.

There was a patter of feet, and Sergeant Abiboo came with four Houssas.

"Take this man," said Sanders, "and put him in irons. To-morrow I will send him down country for judgment."

He walked back to the table, when the men had gone with their prisoner, carefully removed the poisoned dish, and made a meal of eggs and bananas, into neither of which is it possible to introduce ground glass without running the risk of instant detection.

Ground glass—glass powdered so fine that it is like precipitated chalk to the touch—is a bad poison, because when it comes in contact with delicate membranes right down inside a man, it lacerates them and he dies, as the bad men of the coast know, and have known for hundreds of years. In the course of time Lataki came before a judge who sat in a big thatched barn of a courthouse, and Lataki brought three cousins, a brother, and a disinterested friend, to swear that Sanders had put the glass in his own "chop" with malice aforethought. In spite of the unanimity of the evidence—the witnesses had no less than four rehearsals in a little hut the night before the trial—the prisoner was sentenced to fifteen years' penal servitude.

Here the matter would have ended, but for the Lulungo people, who live far away in the north, and who chose to regard the imprisonment of their man as a *casus belli*.

They were a suspicious people, a sullen, loveless, cruel people, and they were geographically favoured, for they lived on the edge of a territory which is indisputably French, and, moreover, unreachable.

Sanders sent flying messages to all the white people who lived within striking distance of the Lulungo. There were six in all, made up of two missions, Jesuit and Baptist. They were most unsatisfactory people, as the following letters show:

The first from the Protestant:

"DEAR MR. COMMISSIONER,—My wife and I are very grateful to you for your warning, but God has called us to this place, and here we must stay, going about our Master's business, until He, in His wisdom, ordains that we shall leave the scene of our labours."

Father Holling wrote:

"DEAR SANDERS,—I think you are wrong about the Lulungo people, several of whom I have seen recently. They are mighty civil, which is the only bad sign I have detected. I shall stay because I think I can fight off any attack they make. I have four Martini-Metford rifles, and three thousand rounds of ammunition, and this house, as you know, is built of stone. I hope you are wrong, but——"

Sanders took his steamboat, his Maxim gun, and his Houssa police, and went up the river, as far as the little stern-wheeler would carry him. At the end of every day's journey he would come to a place where the forest had been cleared, and where, stacked on the beach, was an orderly pile of wood. Somewhere in the forest was a village whose contribution to the State this ever-replenished wood-pile was. Night and day two sounding men with long rods, sitting at the steamer's bow, "stubbed" the water monotonously. Shoal, sandbank, channel, shoal. Sometimes, with a shuddering jar, the boat would slide along the flat surface of a hidden bank, and go flop into the deep water on the other side; sometimes, in the night, the boat would jump a bank to find itself in a little "lake" from which impassable ridges of hidden sand barred all egress. Then the men would slip over the sides of the vessel and walk the sandy floor of the river, pushing the steamer into deep water. When sixty miles from the Baptist Mission, Sanders got news from a friendly native:

"Lord, the Lulungo came at early morning, taking away the missionary, his wife, and his daughter, to their city."

Sanders, yellow with fever, heavy-eyed from want of sleep, unshaven and grimy, wiped the perspiration from his head with the back of his hand.

"Take the steamer up the river," he said to Abiboo. "I must sleep."

He was awakened at four o'clock in the afternoon by the smashing of a water-bottle, which stood on a shelf by his bunk. It smashed for no apparent reason, and he was sprinkled with bits of glass and gouts of water.

Then he heard a rifle go "pang!" close at hand, and as he sprang up and opened the wire-woven door of his cabin, Abiboo came to report.

"There were two men firing from the bank," he said. "One I have shot."

They were nearing the village now, and turning a sharp bend of the river they came in sight of it, and the little *Zaire's* siren yelled and squealed defiantly.

Sanders saw a crowd of men come down to the beach, saw the glitter of spears, and through his glasses the paint on the bodies of the men. Then six canoes came racing out to meet the steamer.

A corporal of Houssas sat down nonchalantly on a little saddle-seat behind the brass Maxim, and gripped its handles.

"Five hundred yards," said Sanders, and the corporal adjusted the sight without perceptible hurry.

The canoes came on at a hurricane speed, for the current was with them. The man behind the gun polished a dull place on the brass water-jacket with the blue sleeves of his coat, and looked up.

Sanders nodded.

The canoes came nearer, one leading the rest in that race where hate nerved effort, and death was the prize.

Suddenly—

"Ha-ha-ha-ha-ha-ha!" laughed the little gun sardonically, and the leading canoe swung round broadside to the stream, because the men who steered it were dead, and half of the oarsmen also.

"Ha-ha-ha-h-a-a!"

There was a wild scramble on the second canoe; it swayed, capsized, and the river was full of black heads, and the air resounded with shrill cries.

As for the remainder of the flotilla it swung round and made for safety; the machine-gun corporal slipped in another belt of cartridges, and made good practice up to nine hundred yards, from which two canoes, frantically paddled, were comparatively safe.

Sanders put his tiny telegraph over to full speed ahead and followed.

On the shore the Lulungo made a stand, and missiles of many kinds struck the little steamer. But the Maxim sprayed the village noisily, and soon there came a nervous man waving a palm leaf, and Sanders ceased firing, and shouted through his megaphone that the messenger must swim aboard.

"Lord, we feel great shame," said the man. He stood in a wet place on the deck, and little rills of water dripped from him. "We did not know we fought Sandi the lion, Sandi the buffalo, before the stamp of whose mighty feet——"

Sanders cut him short.

"There is a white man, a white woman, and a young girl in your city," he said. "Bring them to the ship, and then I will sit in the palaver-house, and talk this matter over."

The man shuffled uneasily.

"Master," he said, "the white man died of the sickness; the woman is ill also; as for the girl, I know nothing."

Sanders looked at him, his head on one side like an inquisitive bird.

"Bring me the white man, alive or dead," he said softly; "also the white woman, well or ill, and the girl."

In an hour they brought the unfortunate missionary, having taken some time to make him look presentable. The wife of the missionary came in another canoe, four women holding her, because she was mad.

"Where is the girl?" asked Sanders. He spoke very little above a whisper.

The messenger made no answer.

"The girl?" said Sanders, and lashed him across the face with his thin stick.

"Master," muttered the man, with his head on his chest, "the chief has her."

Sanders took a turn up and down the deck, then he went to his cabin and came out with two revolvers belted to his hips.

"I will go and see this chief," he said. "Abiboo, do you run the boat's nose into the soft sand of the bank, covering the street with the Maxim whilst I go ashore."

He landed without opposition; neither gun banged nor spear flew as he walked swiftly up the broad street. The girl lay before the chiefs hut quite dead, very calm, very still. The hand to cut short her young life had been more merciful than Sanders dared hope. He lifted the child in his arms, and carried her back to the ship. Once he heard a slight noise behind him, but three rifles crashed from the ship, and he heard a thud and a whimper of pain.

He brought the body on board, and laid it reverently on the little after-deck. Then they told him that the woman had died, and he nodded his head slowly, saying it was better so.

The *Zaire* backed out into mid-stream, and Sanders stood watching the city wistfully. He wanted the chief of the Lulungo badly; he wanted, in his cold rage, to stake him out in spread-eagle fashion, and kill him with slow fires. But the chief and his people were in the woods, and there were the French territories to fly to.

In the evening he buried the missionary and his family on a little island, then drove downstream, black rage in his soul, and a sense of his impotence, for you cannot fight a nation with twenty Houssa policemen.

He came to a little "wooding" at dusk, and tied up for the night. In the morning he resumed his journey, and at noon he came, without a moment's warning, into the thick of a war fleet.

There was no mistaking the character of the hundred canoes that came slowly up-stream four abreast, paddling with machine-like regularity. That line on the right were Akasava men; you could tell that by the blunt noses of the dug-outs. On the left were the Ochori; their canoes were streaked with red cornwood. In the centre, in lighter canoes of better make, he saw the white-barred faces of the Isisi people.

"In the name of heaven!" said Sanders, with raised eyebrows.

There was consternation enough in the fleet, and its irregular lines wavered and broke, but the *Zaire* went steaming into the midst of them. Then Sanders stopped his engines, and summoned the chiefs on board.

"What shame is this?" said Sanders.

Otako, of the Isisi, king and elder chief, looked uncomfortably to Ebeni of Akasava, but it was Bosambo, self-appointed ruler of the Ochori, who spoke.

"Lord," he said, "who shall escape the never-sleeping eye of Sandi? Lo! we thought you many miles away, but like the owl——"

"Where do you go?" asked Sanders.

"Lord, we will not deceive you," said Bosambo. "These great chiefs are my brothers, because certain Lulungo have come down upon our villages and done much harm, stealing and killing. Therefore, because we have suffered equally, and are one in misfortune, we go up against the Lulungo people, for we are human, and our hearts are sore."

A grin, a wicked, mirthless grin, parted Sanders' lips.

"And you would burn and slay?" he asked.

"Master, such was the pleasure we had before us."

"Burning the city and slaying the chief, and scattering the people who hide in the forest?"

"Lord, though they hide in hell we will find them," said Bosambo; "yet, if you, who are as a father to us all, say 'nay,' we will assemble our warriors and tell them it is forbidden."

Sanders thought of the three new graves on a little island.

"Go!" he said, pointing up the river.

He stood on the deck of the *Zaire* and watched the last canoe as it rounded the bend, and listened to the drone of many voices, growing fainter and fainter, singing the Song of the Slayer, such as the Isisi sing before action.

THE END.

FOOTNOTES:

[1] There is a tremendous amount of free hydrocyanic acid (prussic acid) in manioc.

[2] Lo Bengola, the King of the Matabele.

[3] Tusks.

[4] Bula Matidi, *i.e.*, "Stone Breaker," is the native name for the Congo Government.

Transcriber's Notes:
hyphenation, spelling and grammar have been preserved as in the original
Page 9, "Chief, said Sanders ==> "Chief," said Sanders
Page 14, Cailbraith ==> Calbraith
Page 107, was simple there ==> was simple--there
Page 110, peace with him ==> peace with him.
Page 140, his lips impatiently ==> his lips impatiently.
Page 145, before the other? ==> before the other;
Page 163, for it we cannot ==> for if we cannot
Page 163, the way we go ==> the way we go.
Page 240, midstream ==> mid-stream [Ed. for consistency]
Page 242, the Matebele rebels ==> the Matabele rebels

[The end of *Sanders of the River* by Edgar Wallace]

Made in the USA
Columbia, SC
04 December 2024

48453959R00087